S0-AFM-735

TASTING
MINNESOTA

Favorite Recipes from the Land of 10,000 Lakes

by Betsy Nelson

photography by Tom Thulen
foreword by Dara Moskowitz Grumdahl

FARCOUNTRY
PRESS

❧ Dedication ❧

I dedicate this book to cooks past: my grandmothers Joyce and Doris, grandfathers Vern and Art, parents Kay and Dennis, who shared wisdom for me to build upon; and to cooks present: my husband Tom, who chops while I stir; and cooks of the future: my children Levi and Lilly, whose cooking I am looking forward to tasting.

ISBN: 978-1-56037-655-2

© 2016 by Farcountry Press
Text © 2016 by Betsy Nelson
Photography © 2016 by Tom Thulen
Back cover: Split Rock Lighthouse, North Shore, photo © 2009 Ben Podolak.
Pages ii and iii: Kayaking Esther Lake, Cook County, photo © 2016 Travis Novitsky.
Page iv: Skiing the Sugar Bush Trail, Grand Portage, photo © 2016 Travis Novitsky.

All rights reserved. This book may not be reproduced in whole or in part by any means (with the exception of short quotes for the purpose of review) without the permission of the publisher.

For more information on our books, write Farcountry Press, P.O. Box 5630, Helena, MT 59604; call (800) 821–3874; or visit www.farcountrypress.com.

Library of Congress Cataloging-in-Publication Data on file.

Produced in the United States of America. Printed in China.

20   19   18   17   16   1   2   3   4   5

contents

Acknowledgments ♋ xii

Foreword ♋ xiii

Introduction ♋ xv

Guidelines for Recipes ♋ xviii

chapter 1: Breakfast & Brunch

Almond French Toast with Roasted Strawberry Jam
   and Brown Sugar Cream ♋ 2

Broccoli and Sun-dried Tomato Quiche ♋ 3

Buttermilk Herb Biscuits and Chorizo-Poblano Gravy ♋ 5

Cheddar Grits with Ham, Kale, and Fried Duck Egg ♋ 6

Gai Gai Thai Breakfast Bowl ♋ 7

Lemon Ricotta Hotcakes ♋ 9

Lutefisk Benedict ♋ 12

Norwegian Pancakes ♋ 14

Okonomiyaki ♋ 15

Pepita Granola ♋ 16

Three Crows Minnesota Flappers ♋ 17

Tofu Veggie Breakfast Tacos ♋ 18

Wild Hare Cuban Breakfast Burritos ♋ 19

Wild Rice and Quinoa Porridge ♋ 20

chapter 2: Appetizers & Snacks

Apple and Smoked Gouda Turnovers ❧ 22

Beer-Battered Squash Blossoms Stuffed with Cheese Curds ❧ 23

Beet Hummus ❧ 24

Braised Pork Belly ❧ 25

Chanterelles à la Greque ❧ 27

Fermented Herb Yogurt Dip ❧ 28

Fried Green Tomatoes with Skillet Sweet Corn Vinaigrette ❧ 29

"Gotta Have It" Chicken Liver Pâté ❧ 32

Lola Refrigerator Pickles ❧ 33

Prairie Bay's BYOB (Build Your Own Bruschetta) ❧ 34

Smoked Trout, Scrambled Eggs, Capers, and Trout Roe
     on Buttered Toast ❧ 37

Soused Herring ❧ 38

Tod Mun Pla: Curried Fish Cakes with Cucumber Salad ❧ 39

Voyageur Brewing Beer Cheese Fondue ❧ 40

chapter 3: Salads & Sides

Bacon-Glazed Brussels Sprouts ⊗ 42

Burdock Mashed Potatoes ⊗ 43

Buttered Popcorn Gnocchi with Port Wine Reduction ⊗ 44

Carrot-Family Slaw with Dill and Cilantro ⊗ 46

Green Goddess Dressing ⊗ 47

Grilled Bean Slaw ⊗ 48

Lemongrass Pork Tenderloin over Mixed Greens ⊗ 50

Minnesota "Nice-oise" Salad with Salmon ⊗ 51

Raw Vegetable Salad with Açai Vinaigrette ⊗ 52

Roasted Beet Salad with Sherry Pepper Vinaigrette ⊗ 53

Roasted Cauliflower with Mint, Golden Raisins,
    Cornichons, and Parmesan ⊗ 55

Roasted Ramps and Watercress with Pumpkin Seed
    Chèvre Medallions ⊗ 56

Roasted Root Vegetables ⊗ 58

Savory Bread Pudding ⊗ 59

Sofrito Potatoes ⊗ 60

Wild Rice Orzotto with Morels, Ramps, and Hazelnuts ⊗ 61

Wild Rice Salad with Maple-Toasted Almonds ⊗ 62

chapter 4: Soups & Stews

Charred Bell Pepper Soup with Chèvre and Balsamic Vinegar ❧ 64

Curried Red Lentil Dhal ❧ 65

Green Gazpacho with Chive Sour Cream ❧ 66

Grilled Corn and Potato Chowder ❧ 69

Lake Superior Trout and Pumpkin Chowder ❧ 70

Roasted Garlic and Nettle Soup ❧ 71

Roasted Squash and Sweet Potato Soup
     with Hazelnut Oil and Saba ❧ 72

Squash and Wild Rice Chili ❧ 73

Tomato-Fennel Soup with "Inside Out" Grilled
     Cheese Sandwiches ❧ 74

Wild Hare Smoky Squash Chowder ❧ 76

chapter 5: Cocktails

Beebopareebop Strawberry Rhubarb Cocktail ✷ 78

Dashfire Bitters "New Fashioned" ✷ 79

Får North Spirits Cucumber Cosmopolitan ✷ 80

Får North Spirits Oak Island Rum Punch ✷ 81

Norseman Strawberry Rhubarb Fizz ✷ 82

Nothing Gold Can Stay ✷ 83

Steady Eddie ✷ 84

chapter 6: Main Courses

Beef Wellington with Swiss Chard and Mushroom Duxelles ✷ 86

Bison Burger ✷ 87

Braised Beef Pot Roast ✷ 88

Braised Duck Legs with Creamy Farro and Orange ✷ 89

Braised Pork Shank Ossobuco with Herb Gremolata
    (Ossobuco di Maiale) ✷ 92

Brined Turkey with Pan Jus and Caramelized Salsify ✷ 94

Cornmeal Sunfish with Pickled Ramp Aioli ✷ 97

Grilled Chicken with Rhubarb Barbecue Sauce ✷ 98

Grilled Minnesota Pork Loin with Sweet Corn Relish ✷ 99

Lamb Chops with Spring Vegetables ✷ 100

Lamb Meatballs with Soft Polenta, Red Pepper Jus,
    and Parsley-Red Onion Salad ✷ 101

Linguine Bianco e Nero ✷ 104

Maple Stout Sloppy Joes ℞ 105

Pepito Ancho Butter and Pumpkin Jam Sandwiches ℞ 106

Pork Loin Katsu with Sesame Basil Pesto and Fingerling
   Potato Confit ℞ 108

Roasted Chicken Thighs with Clams, Rapini,
   and Dill Mayonnaise ℞ 110

Salmon and Cheddar Quiche ℞ 112

Seared Duck Breast and Amarena Cherries ℞ 114

Sommer Pasta ℞ 116

Surly Bender Braised Short Ribs ℞ 117

Sweet Crispy Beef with Coriander Seed (Nuea Dat Deow) ℞ 118

Venison Tenderloin with Miso Sauce ℞ 119

Walleye with Sesame Crust and Ginger-Orange Teriyaki ℞ 120

chapter 6: Desserts & Sweet Treats

Apple-Ginger Bread Pudding ℞ 122

Beer and Bacon Caramel Sundae ℞ 123

Blueberry Bars with Lemon-Thyme Shortbread Crust ℞ 124

Buttered Popcorn Pot de Crème ℞ 126

Cherry Pecan Scones ℞ 128

Chestnut Crème Brûlée with Cognac-Marinated Prunes ℞ 129

Cranberry-Orange Bread ℞ 131

Ginger Ginger Cookies ℞ 132

Goat Cheese, Honey, Date, and Pistachio Truffles   ✵   133

Honey-Vanilla Cheesecake with Blueberry Caramel Sauce   ✵   135

Mascarpone No-Bake Cheesecake with Chocolate-
    Graham Soil   ✵   137

Molten Chocolate Cakes with Beer Ice Cream   ✵   139

Plum Frangipane Tart   ✵   140

Raspberry Galette   ✵   142

Rosemary Rhubarb Jam   ✵   143

Surly Furious Chocolate Bundt Cake   ✵   144

Sweet Corn Rice Pudding   ✵   145

Whiskey Honey Cake with Whiskey Whipped Cream Filling   ✵   146

Sources for Specialty Ingredients   ✵   147

Contributors   ✵   148

Index   ✵   151

acknowledgments

by Betsy Nelson

When a person takes on a project such as a book meant to showcase the full spectrum of the food scene in her beloved state, it can be daunting. But once I started reaching out for support, it became clear that I was not doing this project all on my own. My husband, Tom Thulen, and I dug into this project just a few weeks after our wedding, and I am immensely grateful for his support. He not only photographed the entire book, but also acted as a gentle taskmaster to help keep this project on schedule. Together we combed Minnesota for known and not-yet-discovered restaurants throughout the state, and are so pleased with the generosity of the chefs and restaurants that were willing to share their recipes with us. I am also very thankful to live in a city that has such a lively food scene. The food cooperatives, farmers' markets, butcher shops, and gourmet shops made the adventure of finding all the ingredients to prepare the recipes all the more enjoyable.

I am most comfortable in the kitchen, surrounded by pots and pans, so when I found myself sitting in front of my computer not knowing how to manage the writing part of the book, I received tremendous support from writer friends Karen Olson, a freelance writer and coach, and Kate Lebo, a writer and author of *Pie School* and *A Commonplace Book of Pie*. Also, my editor, Will Harmon, was incredibly patient with me, and he was available to answer all my questions, no matter how small.

Minnesota is blessed with many cookbook authors, and during my writing process I was fortunate to cross paths with Amy Thielen (*The New Midwestern Table*), Zoë François (*Artisan Bread in Five Minutes a Day*), Robin Asbell (*Big Vegan*, *The Whole Grain Promise*, and others), Brenda Langton (*The Café Brenda Cookbook* and *Spoonriver Cookbook*), Stephanie A. Meyer (*Twin Cities Chef's Table*), and Jenny Breen (*Cooking Up the Good Life*). It feels great to be part of such a supportive community. I was also so happy to have supportive friends and family nearby who were happy to help eat all the food I prepared while testing the recipes. Much appreciation goes to my children, Levi and Lilly, who were forgiving of me during "chaos in the kitchen" days. Thanks to all for your warm hearts and healthy appetites!

foreword

by Dara Moskowitz Grumdahl

People are always telling me to journal. You'll remember more, you'll make sense of your life, you'll never regret keeping a journal, they say. Earnestly. Well guess what. I'm busy. Work, kids, the garden, the restaurants, and sometimes foot after foot of snow falls and I have to shovel out the garbage cans in the alley.

Journal? You don't know how lucky you are that I even remember I'm forgetting to journal.

Then, in the way that fortune so often provides for its greatest fools, Betsy Nelson came along and wrote down the details of the every days of us northern food lovers. Here it is, *Tasting Minnesota*, the journal I wish I had been keeping all these years.

The recipe for Kris Petcharawises' Gai Gai Thai Breakfast Bowl is so many mornings when my kids were tiny, we'd park nearby, duck down the alley to the postage stamp–sized Kingfield farmer's market and find a wonderland of treasures. Would they spend their little cache of farmer's market spending money on tiny pumpkins, or a fist–sized rhubarb pie, or on balloon animals? They'd clutch their $2, and I'd follow them at a safe distance, holding just at my chest a Gai Gai Thai bowl, breathing in the steam, and, when it cooled, forking up bites of an omelet of such lightness and bedecked and beribboned with so many herbal and savory surprises that I felt I could get through anything—even a popped balloon animal. I never thought to journal those beautiful, hectic, fleeting farmer's market mornings—but Betsy wrote them down for me.

On another page of this book: Corner Table's Chanterelles a la Greque. I remembered the first night I met those mushrooms, it was years ago, when I had a newborn and a toddler, both given to howling. New friends had taken me out to give me a pep talk that everything was going to be okay, and we were luxuriating in rare wines while they told me about their unspeakably glamorous world–travels, and also the time their sons almost went through the front picture window. I left that night feeling so hopeful —my babies would sleep through the night one day, and so would I. Also,

wonderfully, I was so cozy-full of mushrooms. Advice that everything is going to be okay does sort of taste like mushrooms. Why hadn't I written that good fact down? I was too tired, and then Betsy rushed in and gave me that memory tied up with a bow.

I could embroider half the recipes in this book with a personal memory. My little one diving behind the bar at Vikre in Duluth, and getting a lesson in how to use an icepick. Celebratory dinners with friends at Spoonriver. Brushing past the path-plantings of thyme at New Scenic, with the slate-scented air streaming in from Lake Superior. We have very specific experiences up here in Minnesota, and we don't talk enough about how specific they are. Here's one fact: We are hundreds of miles from anything, 400-some miles from Chicago, we're farther from Chicago than London, England, is from Paris, France. If that's far enough in Europe to acknowledge a whole other culture, why isn't far enough here? We do things differently here. Our fish come from fresh water, not salt. We go away in the summer, to the lake, or the cabin—a singular place we all sort of share separately. What do we do at the lake? We fish, and perhaps make something like Alan Bergo's Cornmeal Sunfish with Pickled Ramp Aioli. We celebrate, sometimes with something like the Salty Tart's bundt cake. Maybe even on our most relaxed days we're too busy, too foolish to write anything down about our very specific life, our very northern, Minnesotan life, spent together and lived as differently from the rest of the country's as England's is from France's. But we are also lucky. Betsy Nelson wrote it all down for us, our days and meals, our big celebrations and castaway farmer's market breakfasts, so we can make sense of our Minnesotan life, and even, when the mood strikes, cook it again.

introduction

I have lived in Minnesota my entire life and have experienced the gamut when it comes to food—the good with the bland, the vibrant with the beige, the fresh with the frozen. The food scene has changed over the past couple of decades. Now we have James Beard Award–winning chefs and restaurants that get mentioned in *Food & Wine* magazine. You can find something to please your palate in every part of the state.

Some visitors from larger coastal cities don't yet believe it. I've seen them pleasantly surprised when they experience the incredible diversity and quality of Minnesotan food. Perhaps their assumptions about bland midwestern food stem from our cold winters and our penchant for heartier comfort food during this season. But having four distinct seasons makes us appreciate all that each has to offer. Minnesota chefs are humble. They don't run around saying "Bam!" or bask in the spotlight alone. Instead, they are quick to share the credit for their success with local farmers and food producers who provide them with quality ingredients.

The trend for supporting local food producers is strong in my home state, as it is nationwide. CSA (community supported agriculture) farms for meats and produce are becoming more and more popular—there are 176 farmers' markets in Minnesota and nearly fifty food cooperatives. Consumers want to know where their food is coming from and spend their dollars locally. Breweries, cideries, and small distilleries are popping up everywhere. Many are tucked into neighborhoods where folks can walk or bike, listen to live music, grab a snack at a food truck, and connect with their neighbors.

I learned about food and cooking through the desire to connect with other people. At a young age, my very first recipe included an immediately available ingredient—snow scooped from the front yard. I stirred in some strawberry syrup and made a quick sweet treat that I shared with my younger brothers. My mom even helped me jot it down on a recipe card so we could make it again. I started as an eager prep cook at home with my mother and grandparents, making corn chowder, beef pot roast,

and apple cake, and soon took the lead role, cooking and cleaning for my grandparents when they were ill. In college, cooking was something I did to get to know people better. I formed friendships with foreign students and broadened my palate over dinner parties where everyone shared cuisine from their respective countries. These meals opened up my thinking about food and culture. We all eat. Food unifies us.

After college I went to work for a series of restaurant kitchens, starting with Chef Lenny Russo, then Brenda Langton, and eventually found myself as the chef at the Aveda Spa and Retreat in Osceola, Wisconsin. But before becoming a professional cook, I was a little Scandinavian American who helped her family prepare traditional foods like rullepolse, krumkake, lefse, and lutefisk.

Lutefisk was one of those foods my brothers and I didn't particularly enjoy, but we ate it dutifully to please my grandfather. After his passing, lutefisk disappeared from our holiday table. It had been years since I had even thought of it. Out of the blue one day, my college roommate, Alejandra, came home with a package of lutefisk she had picked up at Ingebretsen's Scandinavian market. She made a dish she learned from her own culinary curiosity, bacalhau, a Portuguese dish with salted cod. It put lutefisk in a whole new light for me, because this dish provided vibrant flavors to an ingredient that had previously been a colorless fishy blob to me.

The process of writing this book has been much like hanging out in the kitchen with friends. Unexpected flavor combinations, hilarious commentary, and personal stories from the contributing chefs made me connect with their recipes even more. The search for recipes to include here will always feel incomplete to me, as there are always new places opening, as well as hidden gems that remain so as of this printing. My hope is that this book will encourage folks to explore every beautiful corner of Minnesota and discover all the great food it has to offer, from the international collection of food at the Midtown Global Market in Minneapolis, to the porketta found in the most humble IGA grocery store up on the Iron Range, to a night at a pizza farm in Northfield. Remember to keep your eyes peeled for pop-up events such as "Dinner on the Farm" and Michelle Gayer's "Power, Corruption, and Pies," or experience Sri Lankan food at a "Curry Diva Dinner" with Chef Heather Jansz.

It is my hope that readers will enjoy cooking new dishes and learning about new restaurants, and that they'll find new friends in the chefs who have so generously shared their recipes with us. Some of the recipes are simple, some are more involved, but there is always something to learn and appreciate about the process of gathering ingredients and cooking. Think of it as the best potluck supper you've ever been to, the great Minnesota get-together.

—BETSY NELSON

guidelines for recipes

❧ Temperatures are listed in degrees Fahrenheit.

❧ Fresh produce should be washed before using.

❧ Garlic, onions, carrots, and potatoes should be peeled before use unless noted otherwise.

❧ All-purpose flour was used in testing any recipe calling for flour unless noted otherwise.

❧ Sugar refers to white granulated sugar unless noted otherwise.

❧ Butter is unsalted butter unless noted otherwise.

❧ Salt is iodized table salt unless noted otherwise.

❧ Pepper refers to freshly ground black pepper.

❧ Recipes were tested using large eggs.

❧ Chile peppers lend flavor to a range of cuisines and almost as many spellings. In this book, *chile* refers to a chile pepper itself or a sauce or oil made from chiles. Spelled as *chili*, it refers to the finished stew or to the spice mixture, chili powder, used as a flavoring. The spelling on product labels at your grocer may vary.

❧ Nuts may be toasted either in the oven or on the stove. Spread nuts in a single layer on a baking sheet and bake at 350 degrees or in a skillet over medium heat until lightly browned and aromatic. Nuts burn quickly once they brown, so watch closely.

Breakfast & Brunch

Norwegian Pancakes, p. 14

Roasted strawberry jam

1 pound strawberries

2 tablespoons sugar

1 lemon, juiced

French toast

3 eggs, beaten

1 cup almond milk

¼ cup almond paste

¼ cup sugar

¼ teaspoon almond extract

2 tablespoons clarified butter

1 loaf challah, sliced ½ inch
    thick (18 to 20 slices)

Brown sugar cream

16 ounces crème fraîche

½ teaspoon vanilla paste

2 tablespoons brown sugar

Serves 8 to 10

Almond French Toast with Roasted Strawberry Jam and Brown Sugar Cream

THE THIRD BIRD, MINNEAPOLIS   ∞   CHEF LUCAS ALMENDINGER

The Third Bird is nested right off Loring Park, just west of downtown Minneapolis. The feather in the hat of this dish is the almond paste in the French toast (using challah, an egg bread), which is crowned by fresh strawberry jam.

Preheat the oven to 375 degrees.

For the roasted strawberry jam:
Wash, core, and quarter the strawberries. Arrange them on a baking sheet and roast until they have released their liquid, 15 to 20 minutes. Taste and adjust the flavor to your liking with sugar and lemon juice. Cool and set aside.

For the French toast:
In a blender, mix the eggs, almond milk, almond paste, sugar, and almond extract until smooth. Preheat a griddle and brush with clarified butter. Dip each slice of challah in the egg mixture and cook on the griddle until golden brown on each side.

For the brown sugar cream:
While the French toast cooks, prepare the brown sugar cream by mixing the crème fraîche, vanilla paste, and brown sugar in a small bowl.

Serve the French toast hot off the griddle topped with the roasted strawberry jam and brown sugar cream.

Crust

⅓ cup salted butter, chilled

1 cup whole wheat pastry flour

2 to 3 tablespoons ice water

Quiche filling

1 tablespoon vegetable oil

1 large onion, coarsely chopped

½ cup chopped fresh mushrooms

1 small head broccoli, chopped, florets and stems separated

1 teaspoon dried rosemary

1 teaspoon dried thyme

½ teaspoon dried sage

½ teaspoon dried parsley

½ teaspoon dried marjoram

½ teaspoon dried basil

¼ teaspoon pepper

6 sun-dried tomato halves, chopped

2 cups grated cheese (a mix of sharp Cheddar, Swiss, and Monterey Jack)

5 eggs

1 cup milk

Serves 8 to 10

Broccoli and Sun-dried Tomato Quiche

SCANDINAVIAN INN, LANESBORO
INNKEEPERS PETER TORKELSON AND VICKI CHAMBARD TORKELSON

This is an easy make-ahead dish that reheats well the next day. Using whole wheat flour not only makes it healthier but adds a nice nutty flavor and texture.

Preheat the oven to 350 degrees.

For the crust:
In a medium mixing bowl, cut the cold butter into the pastry flour until it is crumbly with pea-size pieces. Add water one tablespoon at a time until the dough is moistened and workable. Press into a 9-inch pie plate to form the bottom crust. Cover and let the dough rest while you prepare the filling.

For the quiche filling:
In a large pan, heat the oil, then add the onions and fry for about 1 minute. Add the mushrooms and cook until onions begin to brown, about 2 more minutes. Add the broccoli stem pieces and cook for another minute. Then add the florets, stir, and cover for 1 minute. Uncover, stir in the herbs and continue to cook for 30 seconds. Remove from heat and stir in the sun-dried tomatoes. Let cool.

Sprinkle one-third of the shredded cheese into the pie shell. Layer in half of the vegetable mixture, favoring the broccoli florets for this middle layer. Add another one-third of the cheese and all but 2 table-spoons of the vegetables, and then add the rest of the cheese. Sprinkle with the remaining 2 tablespoons of vegetables.

In a bowl, whisk the eggs and milk together and pour slowly over the vegetables and cheese in the pie shell. Bake for 1 hour and 15 minutes, or until no longer jiggly. Remove from the oven and allow to stand at least 5 to 10 minutes before cutting. Serve warm.

Buttermilk herb biscuits

2 cups flour

2 teaspoons baking powder

1 teaspoon sea salt

½ teaspoon baking soda

¼ cup chopped fresh parsley

¼ cup chopped scallions

½ cup (1 stick) cold butter,
    cut into ½-inch cubes

1 cup cold buttermilk

Chorizo-poblano gravy

2 tablespoons vegetable shortening

2 pounds ground chorizo sausage

½ cup diced (¼ inch) onion

4 cloves garlic, minced

3 tablespoons flour

2 cups heavy cream

1 cup chicken stock

2 poblano peppers, charred,
    skin and seeds removed,
    ½-inch dice

Salt and pepper to taste

Serves 8

Buttermilk Herb Biscuits and Chorizo-Poblano Gravy

BREAKING BREAD CAFÉ, MINNEAPOLIS
CHEF LACHELLE CUNNINGHAM

Chef Cunningham is passionate about cooking global comfort food. Her twist on classic biscuits and gravy includes fresh herbs, spicy chorizo sausage, and poblano peppers.

Place the oven rack in the center and preheat the oven to 425 degrees. Line a baking sheet with parchment paper.

For the biscuits:
Whisk the flour, baking powder, salt, baking soda, and chopped herbs together in a large bowl. Add the butter cubes and toss to coat them in the flour mixture. Place the bowl in the freezer for 10 minutes, then cut the butter into the flour mixture until the butter pieces are pea-size. Drizzle in the buttermilk and stir just enough for the shaggy dough to come together. Scrape the dough out onto a floured work surface and dust the top with more flour. Using floured hands, gently pat the dough into a 1-inch-thick circle. Dip a 2½-inch circular cutter in flour and cut eight biscuits. Transfer to the lined baking sheet, spacing at least an inch apart. Bake until the biscuits are golden brown on top, about 15 minutes.

For the chorizo-poblano gravy:
Heat the vegetable shortening in a pot over medium-high heat and add the chorizo, onions, and garlic. Cook until the chorizo is cooked through. Stir in the flour, reduce heat to medium, and cook for 3 to 4 minutes. In a small pot over medium heat, stir together the cream and chicken stock, then add to the pan with the chorizo. Reduce heat to simmer for 20 minutes, stirring as the gravy thickens. Stir in the poblano peppers and season with salt and pepper.

To assemble:
Split the biscuits in half, plate, and top with gravy. Serve immediately.

8 cups cold water

2 cups hominy grits

¾ cup (1½ sticks) butter, divided

2 cups shredded white
    Cheddar cheese

Tabasco sauce to taste

Salt and pepper to taste

4 tablespoons thinly sliced shallots

2 tablespoons thinly sliced garlic

2 bunches lacinato kale,
    washed and roughly chopped

1 pound Red Table Meats
    country ham, sliced and
    cut into thin strips

6 duck eggs

Serves 6

Cheddar Grits with Ham, Kale, and Fried Duck Egg

THE KENWOOD RESTAURANT, MINNEAPOLIS
CHEF DON SAUNDERS

The Kenwood is tucked into a cozy neighborhood near Lake of the Isles. This dish is comfort food at its finest. The cheesy grits create a happy home for the salty ham and garlicky kale. A simple fried duck egg is the crowning glory. This recipe calls for hominy grits, which should be soaked overnight to reduce cooking time.

In a large pot, add the water and grits and let soak overnight.

Skim off any husks that floated to the top of the water, place the pot over medium heat, and bring to a boil. Reduce to a simmer and cook, stirring often, until the grits are tender, about 45 minutes. Stir in ½ cup (1 stick) of the butter, the cheese, and a few drops of Tabasco sauce, and season with salt and pepper to taste. Keep warm.

In a large pot, melt 2 tablespoons of the butter, add the shallots and garlic, and sweat on medium-low for about 5 minutes, stirring often. Add the kale and a few pinches of salt. Cover and cook over medium heat until the kale is tender, about 20 minutes.

In a large sauté pan, heat the kale and ham together. In a separate sauté pan, melt the remaining 2 tablespoons of butter and fry the duck eggs sunny side up, one at a time.

Place a serving of grits on each plate and top with the kale and ham. Top each with a fried duck egg and serve immediately.

Rice

2 cups uncooked jasmine rice

2 cups water

Curry sauce

1 can coconut milk

2 ounces green curry paste

2 tablespoons palm sugar
    or granulated sugar

Carrot slaw

6 to 8 cloves garlic, peeled

8 to 10 Thai chiles

2 cups grated or julienned carrots

4 tablespoons fish sauce

1 to 2 limes, juiced

Sautéed chicken

2 tablespoons vegetable oil

1 pound ground free-range chicken

3 tablespoons sweet soy sauce

2 tablespoons fish sauce

1 cup Thai basil leaves

Gai Gai Thai Breakfast Bowl

GAI GAI THAI, MINNEAPOLIS
CHEF AND OWNER KRIS PETCHARAWISES

Savory smells and a friendly smile draw you in for a delicious rice bowl from Gai Gai Thai, a mobile kitchen found at farmers' markets around the Twin Cities. Chef Petcharawises uses free-range chicken from Kadejan.

For the rice:
Rinse and drain the rice three times. Place the rice and 2 cups of water in a rice cooker and set to cook.

For the curry sauce:
While the rice is cooking, heat the coconut milk in a small saucepan, then whisk in the curry paste and sugar to mix well. Keep warm.

For the carrot slaw:
With a mortar and pestle or food processor, blend the garlic and chiles until a paste forms. In a medium bowl, mix half of the garlic–chile paste with the carrots, 4 tablespoons of fish sauce, and lime juice.

For the sautéed chicken:
Heat the vegetable oil in a large sauté pan. Stir in the remaining garlic–chile paste and heat for a minute or two. Add the chicken, soy sauce, and fish sauce and cook completely. Add the Thai basil leaves and set aside.

For the Thai omelet:
In a bowl, beat the eggs with the fish sauce. Heat the vegetable oil in a large omelet pan and pour in the beaten egg mixture. Flash fry on high heat, flipping once, and cook until the eggs are set.

(continued on page 8)

Thai omelet

4 organic eggs, beaten

4 teaspoons fish sauce

¼ cup vegetable oil

Garnish

½ cup chopped green onions

½ cup fried onions

½ cup sliced red bell pepper

Serves 4 to 6

To assemble:
Cut the omelet into four to six portions. Divide the rice into bowls and top each serving with carrot slaw, sautéed chicken, Thai omelet, and green curry sauce. Garnish with green onions, fried onions, and peppers and serve immediately.

½ cup sugar, divided

4 tablespoons freshly grated
lemon zest

1 tablespoon fresh lemon juice

6 egg whites

9 egg yolks

⅓ cup sweet cream butter, melted

1 cup whole milk ricotta cheese

1 teaspoon kosher salt

⅓ cup flour

Extra sweet cream butter, melted,
for cooking hotcakes

2 cups assorted fresh berries
(blackberries, raspberries,
blueberries, and strawberries)

Powdered sugar for dusting

Makes 16 hotcakes

Lemon Ricotta Hotcakes

HELL'S KITCHEN, MINNEAPOLIS
CHEFS MITCH OMER AND ANN BAUER

Chef Omer served these hotcakes to 600 folks in the town of Embarrass at a fund-raiser for the local fire department. The mercury dipped to 37 degrees below zero that February morning. He and his staff made gallons upon gallons of the batter, and volunteers worked the griddles. You too will find these cakes a great comfort on a chilly winter morning!

In a medium saucepan, mix ¼ cup of the sugar with the lemon zest and juice. Bring to a boil over medium-high heat, then reduce to a simmer and cook, stirring frequently, for 7 minutes. Remove from heat and allow to cool to room temperature.

Pour the egg whites into the bowl of a stand mixer fitted with a wire whisk and whisk on high until firm peaks form. Reduce the speed to low and slowly add the egg yolks, one at a time. Whisk until well blended, about 1 minute.

With the mixer on low, slowly add the melted butter until incorporated into the batter. Add the remaining ¼ cup of sugar, the ricotta cheese, lemon zest mixture, and salt. Whisk on medium for 1 minute. Reduce the speed to low again and gradually add the flour. Continue mixing for 1 minute. Stop the mixer and scrape the sides and bottom of the bowl with a rubber spatula. Return the mixer to medium speed and mix until the batter is smooth with no lumps, about 1 more minute. It is best to refrigerate the batter for a few hours prior to making the hotcakes, and even better to refrigerate it overnight. Store in a container with a tight-fitting lid until ready to cook; it will keep well for up to 3 days.

(continued on page 10)

When you are ready to cook the hotcakes, stir the mixture well. Preheat a large skillet or griddle over medium-high heat. Brush the skillet generously with melted butter and scoop ¼-cup portions of batter onto the griddle, leaving 2 inches between each hotcake to allow them to spread. Cook until bubbles appear throughout the batter and the bottom is golden brown, about 5 minutes. Flip the hotcakes over and cook for another 3 to 5 minutes. Serve with fresh berries and a dusting of powdered sugar.

Lutefisk roll

2 tablespoons butter, softened

1 pound lutefisk, soaked according
    to package directions

4 fresh bay leaves

8 ounces whitefish fillet, skinned,
    pin bones removed

1 tablespoon fresh thyme leaves,
    destemmed

1 tablespoon hot sauce

1 tablespoon fish sauce

1 tablespoon salt

2 teaspoons pepper

3 egg whites

¼ cup minced fresh chives

2 tablespoons vegetable oil

Bacon and arugula sauce

½ cup bacon lardons,
    or thick-cut bacon,
    cut into small strips

2 cups arugula

¼ cup heavy cream

1 tablespoon Dijon mustard

Poached eggs

1 tablespoon white wine vinegar

6 large eggs, the freshest available

Serves 6

Lutefisk Benedict

LAKE AVENUE RESTAURANT, DULUTH   ❧   CHEF TONY BERAN

Lutefisk, a traditional Scandinavian food whose popularity seems to be fading (unlike its aroma), presents the ultimate culinary challenge. Chef Tony created this recipe as a tribute to his Swedish grandpa, Harold Carlson. Plan to cook the lutefisk a day ahead of time and then air-dry it in a refrigerator.

Preheat the oven to 350 degrees.

For the lutefisk roll:
Line a rimmed baking sheet with aluminum foil and rub entire surface of the foil with the softened butter. Pat the lutefisk dry with paper towels and place on the buttered foil. Tear the bay leaves into small pieces and scatter over the lutefisk. Cover with another sheet of buttered foil and bake for 30 minutes.

Remove the lutefisk from the oven and remove the top layer of foil. Drain any liquid and return to the oven uncovered. Bake for another 10 to 15 minutes, removing every 5 minutes to drain off more liquid. Remove from the oven, discard the bay leaves, and place the sheet in the refrigerator to air-dry the lutefisk overnight. This is best done in a beer fridge if you have one!

The next day, preheat the oven to 400 degrees.

In a food processor, combine the lutefisk, whitefish, thyme, hot sauce, fish sauce, salt, and pepper. Process for a couple minutes, then scrape down the sides, add the egg whites and the chives, and process until just combined. Spoon the mixture onto a large sheet of plastic wrap. (Use a polyethylene-based wrap such as Saran Wrap or Glad Cling-Wrap. Do not use PVC-based wrap.) Roll up into a tube about 3 inches in diameter, twisting the ends tight, like a Tootsie Roll. Wrap the tube in several more layers of plastic wrap to make it nice and stable. Next, wrap the plastic tube in two layers of aluminum foil, again twisting the ends tight.

Place the tube of lutefisk in a deep baking dish or Dutch oven and cover completely with cold water. Place in the oven and cook for 1 hour.

Fill a large, deep pan with cold water and ice cubes. Carefully remove the baking dish from the oven, then use tongs to remove the lutefisk roll and place it, still wrapped, in the ice water bath. Chill for at least 20 minutes. When chilled, place the lutefisk roll on a cutting board and remove the foil and plastic wrap. Trim the ends and cut the roll into six equal slices.

In a nonstick pan, heat the vegetable oil and sear the lutefisk slices 2 minutes on each side. Remove the seared lutefisk, placing each slice on its own plate.

For the bacon and arugula sauce:
Using the same pan, cook the bacon. Add the arugula and stir until wilted. Add the cream and mustard and reduce heat to low. Simmer to thicken the sauce.

For the poached eggs:
Fill a nonstick pan with 1½ inches of water, bring to just a simmer, and add the vinegar. Carefully crack an egg and ease it into the hot water; repeat for the remaining eggs. Poach for 4½ minutes and remove with a slotted spoon.

To assemble:
Divide the bacon–arugula mixture onto each of the lutefisk slices and top with a poached egg. Serve immediately.

❧ *Note: Lutefisk from Olsen's Fish Company in Minneapolis does not require soaking.*

4 eggs

2 cups whole milk, divided

1 ½ cups flour

½ teaspoon salt

4 tablespoons sugar

2 tablespoons butter, melted

Lingonberry preserves

Maple syrup

Whipped cream

Powdered sugar

Makes 16 thin pancakes

Norwegian Pancakes

MAPLELAG RESORT, CALLAWAY   ❧   CHEF DEB OLK

These lacy cakes have fortified many skiers as they blaze the trails through the woods at Maplelag. Dress them up as you like with lingonberry preserves, real maple syrup, and, if you're feeling fancy, whipped cream.

In a large bowl, beat the eggs, add 1 cup of the milk, and mix. In a separate bowl, combine the flour, salt, and sugar and then add the dry ingredients to the egg mixture, beating until smooth. Stir in the remaining milk and melted butter.

Heat and lightly grease a griddle, and pour about ¼ cup of pancake batter for each cake onto the griddle. Flip the pancakes when the batter on top begins to set up, and cook until golden brown on each side.

Serve with lingonberry preserves or fresh berries, maple syrup, whipped cream, and a dusting of powdered sugar.

Pancakes

5 eggs, beaten

1 ⅓ cups chicken stock

2 cups flour

1 teaspoon salt

8 cups finely shredded cabbage

8 scallions, thinly sliced, white part only, greens reserved

4 tablespoons vegetable oil, divided

6 slices bacon, cut in half lengthwise

Toppings

1 cup mayonnaise

1 to 2 tablespoons apple cider vinegar

Reserved green scallion tops, sliced into thin strips

1 carrot, peeled and julienned

Makes 4 large pancakes

Okonomiyaki

ELEPHANT WALK BED AND BREAKFAST, STILLWATER
CHEF AND OWNER RITA GRAYBILL

Inspired by her world travels, Chef Graybill offers a variety of comforting and adventuresome dishes for her guests. Okonomiyaki is a Japanese pancake. Cabbage in a pancake may sound unusual, but it is a guest favorite. This recipe can be adapted in many ways, as it is in Japan. It's served kind of like a pizza, with many varieties of toppings, so it's a great opportunity to explore in the kitchen.

For the pancakes:
In a large bowl, whisk the eggs with the chicken stock, flour, and salt until smooth. Stir in the cabbage and scallions.

In a large, nonstick skillet, heat 1 tablespoon of the vegetable oil. When the oil is hot, add one-quarter of the cabbage mixture to the skillet and press the cabbage down into the batter to spread the pancake out. Arrange three half slices of the bacon on the pancake batter and press in with a spatula. Cook the pancake until golden on one side, 3 to 4 minutes, and then flip over and cook the other side until done. (To facilitate turning the pancake, turn it onto a plate once the first side has cooked—the pancake will be firm enough to release from the plate. Then turn it onto another plate and flip it back into the pan to cook the other side.) Repeat this process with the remaining batter.

For the toppings:
While the pancakes are cooking, whisk the mayonnaise and apple cider vinegar together and pour into a squirt bottle or pastry tube. If you don't have either of those, put the sauce into a resealable plastic bag and cut a small hole in a corner of the bag to pipe the sauce onto the pancakes.

Scatter the tops of the pancakes with the julienned scallion tops and carrots and serve immediately.

❧ **Note:** *For flavor options, substitute 1 ½ cups of shrimp or crumbled breakfast sausage for the bacon.*

3 cups old-fashioned rolled oats

3 cups frosted cornflakes cereal

1 cup coconut flakes

1 cup pepitas (shelled pumpkin
    seeds)

½ cup powdered milk

2 tablespoons corn flour

1 tablespoon salt

¼ cup honey

½ cup maple syrup

1 cup brown sugar, firmly packed

¼ cup sunflower seed oil
    or other neutral oil

2 teaspoons vanilla extract

Makes 8 cups

Pepita Granola

HOLA AREPA, MINNEAPOLIS   ❧   CHEF HEATHER KIM

This addictively snackable granola may become your new favorite. Hola Arepa serves this with their yogurt flan, but you can scatter it over a bowl of yogurt or just nibble it right out of the jar.

Preheat the oven to 325 degrees and line two baking sheets with parchment paper.

In a large bowl, combine the oats, cornflakes, coconut flakes, pepitas, powdered milk, corn flour, and salt and toss to mix. Distribute the mix evenly onto the baking sheets.

In a medium saucepan, bring the honey, maple syrup, brown sugar, and oil to a boil. Remove from heat and stir in the vanilla extract. Pour the sugar mixture evenly over the dry ingredients on the sheet trays and mix with a spatula to distribute well. Bake for 20 minutes, mixing again with a spatula after 10 minutes to ensure even baking.

Remove the granola from the oven when it is a deep golden color. Spread the granola onto a clean sheet of parchment to cool completely. If you want larger chunks of granola, allow it to cool undisturbed on the baking sheet. Granola will become more crunchy after it has cooled. Store in airtight containers at room temperature for up to a week or in the freezer for a month.

❧ *Note: This recipe can be easily varied by substituting your favorite cereal for the frosted flakes or using peanuts, cashews, or other nuts in place of the pepitas.*

Dry pancake mix

4 cups whole wheat flour

1 cup buckwheat flour

⅓ cup soy flour

1 cup instant nonfat dry milk

1 tablespoon salt

1½ tablespoons baking powder

½ cup sugar

¾ cup solid vegetable shortening

Flappers

1 cup dry pancake mix

½ cup water

4 tablespoons cooked wild rice

4 tablespoons fresh blueberries

Toppings

Maple syrup

Fresh blueberries

Makes 4 pancakes

Three Crows Minnesota Flappers

THREE CROWS, DELANO OWNER GINA COBURN

Childhood memories of picking wild blueberries at her grandparents' farm and eating wild rice harvested by her father inspired Gina to create these hearty cakes. They are easy to whip up when you make the mix ahead of time.

For the dry pancake mix:
Mix the dry ingredients together in a large bowl. Using a pastry blender or your hands, work the shortening into the dry ingredients until it is the consistency of coarse cornmeal. This makes about 7 cups of dry pancake mix. Seal the mix in an airtight container and store in the pantry for up to a month, or in the refrigerator or freezer for six months.

For the flappers:
In a small bowl, stir ½ cup of water into 1 cup of the dry pancake mix. If the batter seems too thick, stir in a bit more water.

Pour ¼ cup of the batter onto a hot, greased griddle. Sprinkle 1 tablespoon of cooked rice and 1 tablespoon of blueberries onto the raw side of the pancake. Cook until the bottom of the pancake is brown and the top is dry and covered with small bubbles. Flip the pancake and brown it on the second side. Repeat with the remaining batter.

Serve with hot maple syrup and blueberries.

Tofu veggie taco filling

2 (14-ounce) blocks extra-firm tofu, crumbled

2 tablespoons vegetable oil

1 onion, chopped

2 tablespoons minced garlic

1 green bell pepper or poblano pepper, finely chopped

1 red bell pepper, finely chopped

1 yellow bell pepper, finely chopped

1 teaspoon grated fresh ginger root

½ teaspoon ground coriander

½ teaspoon ground cumin

1½ teaspoons ground turmeric

1 (15-ounce) can black beans, rinsed and drained

¼ cup chopped cilantro

Salt and pepper to taste

12 to 16 corn tortillas

Garnish

1 (16-ounce) jar salsa

2 avocados, diced

2 cups grated Cheddar cheese

1 bunch scallions, chopped

Hot sauce

Serves 6 to 8

Tofu Veggie Breakfast Tacos

BREAKING BREAD CAFÉ, MINNEAPOLIS
CHEF LACHELLE CUNNINGHAM

Surrounded by fast-food restaurants, Breaking Bread offers healthy comfort food that nourishes the local community in more ways than one. The café got its start through Appetite for Change, a nonprofit that works to revitalize depressed neighborhoods by using food as a tool for building health, wealth, and social change. If you're unsure about tofu, these zesty tacos will win you over!

Preheat the oven to 350 degrees.

Lightly oil a baking sheet and roast the tofu crumbles for 20 minutes to remove excess water.

Heat the oil in a large skillet and sauté the onion, garlic, and peppers until softened, about 4 minutes. Stir in the ginger, coriander, and cumin and cook until fragrant, about 1 minute. Stir in the tofu and then the turmeric and mix so the tofu is colored by the turmeric. Add the beans and cook until heated through. Stir in the cilantro and season with salt and pepper.

Warm the tortillas on a hot skillet. Serve the tortillas, filling, and garnishes buffet style.

Chili

3 tablespoons olive oil

1 onion, diced fine (about 1 cup)

2 cups finely diced mixed
    vegetables

3 cloves garlic, minced

1 teaspoon ground cumin

1 teaspoon chili powder

1 teaspoon smoked Spanish paprika

2 to 3 tablespoons water

1 (15-ounce) can black beans,
    drained and rinsed

1 (15-ounce) can diced tomatoes

Salt and pepper to taste

Cheesy scrambled eggs

6 eggs

2 teaspoons water

Pinch each salt and pepper

6 ounces shredded Cheddar cheese

Presentation

6 (8-inch) flour tortillas

Salsa

Sour cream

Bunch scallions, chopped

Serves 6

Wild Hare Cuban Breakfast Burritos

WILD HARE BISTRO, BEMIDJI
CHEF AND OWNER MONI SCHNEIDER

A hearty breakfast that is packed with fresh veggies and flavor is a great way to start the day. Change up the veggies in this chili mixture with whatever is in season—a mix of carrots, peppers, squash, and sweet potatoes works well. Cook it the night before to make your morning breakfast prep easier.

For the chili:
Heat the olive oil in a sauté pan, add the onions with a pinch of salt, and sauté until they soften and begin to brown. Stir in the diced vegetables, garlic, spices, and water. Cover and simmer until soft, about 10 minutes. Stir in the black beans and tomatoes, simmering gently to heat through. Season to taste with salt and pepper and keep warm.

For the cheesy scrambled eggs:
Whisk the eggs in a small bowl with 2 teaspoons of water and a pinch of salt and pepper. Stir in the shredded Cheddar cheese. Pour into a nonstick pan over medium heat and cook, stirring until just set. (Alternatively, you can "scramble" the eggs in the microwave, stirring at 30–second intervals, until set.)

To assemble:
Warm the tortillas briefly in a dry nonstick pan in the oven, or microwave on a plate. Fill each with chili and cheesy scrambled eggs and roll into a burrito. Top with your favorite salsa, sour cream, and chopped scallions.

Wild rice and quinoa porridge

1 ½ cups cooked wild rice

1 cup cooked brown rice

1 cup cooked quinoa

1 ½ cups milk

½ cup heavy cream

¼ cup brown sugar

½ teaspoon ground cinnamon

¼ teaspoon ground ginger

¼ cup maple syrup

¼ cup dried cranberries

¼ teaspoon kosher salt

Garnish

½ cup whipped cream

Dash vanilla extract

¼ cup toasted walnuts

Serves 4

Wild Rice and Quinoa Porridge

LOLA—AN AMERICAN BISTRO, NEW ULM
CHEF AND OWNER LACEY LUETH

This is not your grandmother's porridge, but it is nonetheless wholesome and comforting with the whole-grain goodness of wild rice, quinoa, and brown rice studded with dried cranberries and sweetened with maple syrup.

For the wild rice and quinoa porridge:
Place all the porridge ingredients together in a 2-quart saucepan and simmer over medium-low heat until thickened, 5 to 10 minutes. Adjust the seasonings as needed.

Serve in bowls topped with a dollop of whipped cream, a splash of vanilla, and toasted walnuts. Leftover porridge keeps well refrigerated. To reheat, add a bit more cream while warming over low heat.

Appetizers & Snacks

Lola Refrigerator Pickles, p. 33

3 baking apples (Haralson
   or Granny Smith)

4 ounces smoked Gouda cheese,
   diced

½ lemon, juiced

1 tablespoon flour

Cayenne pepper to taste

2 puff pastry sheets, thawed

Chili powder for dusting
   tops of tarts

Makes 24 small turnovers

Apple and Smoked Gouda Turnovers

KITCHEN IN THE MARKET, MINNEAPOLIS
CHEF AND CO-OWNER MOLLY HERRMANN

Crisp autumn days bring our thoughts to orchard visits and baking something lovely. Buttery pastry filled with sweet apples, smoked Gouda, and a hint of cayenne is just right for when the leaves turn color.

Preheat the oven to 400 degrees. Line a baking sheet with parchment paper.

Peel, core, and dice the apples. In a large bowl, combine the apples, cheese, lemon juice, flour, and cayenne and mix to coat.

Cut each puff pastry sheet into twelve squares for twenty-four squares total. Place a tablespoon or more of filling in the center of each puff pastry square. Dab two edges of each square with water and fold the opposite edges over the filling to form a triangle. Crimp the edges to seal. Place the turnovers onto the baking sheet and dust the tops with chili powder. Bake until the turnovers are golden brown and flaky, 15 to 20 minutes.

Beer-Battered Squash Blossoms Stuffed with Cheese Curds

THAT FOOD GIRL, MINNEAPOLIS BETSY NELSON

Boost cheese curds up a notch by tucking them into the golden blossom of a zucchini, pumpkin, or other squash plant. Use only the male blossoms, which grow farther from the vine on longer stems. They don't produce fruits. Rather, they are there for fertilization, far outnumbering the female blossoms. Find blossoms at the farmers' market if you aren't growing squashes.

4 cups vegetable oil for frying

16 male squash blossoms
    with 2-inch stems

8 ounces cheese curds

1 ¼ cups flour

1 teaspoon kosher salt

12 ounces chilled lager-style beer

½ cup minced fresh chives

Makes 16 blossoms

Preheat the frying oil in a large skillet to 350 degrees.

Remove the stamen from the center of each blossom. Fill with one or two cheese curds, or as many as will comfortably fit and still allow the petals to wrap around the curds. Set the stuffed blossoms on a tray while you prepare the batter.

Working quickly, whisk the flour, salt, and beer together, being mindful of not overmixing as this will deflate the batter. Fold in the chives. Dip one blossom at a time, grasping both ends and rolling gently through the batter to coat evenly. Carefully slip the battered blossoms into the hot oil and fry until golden brown, turning once to cook each side.

Remove the fried blossoms onto a tray covered with paper towel to absorb excess oil. Repeat until all the blossoms are cooked.

⌧ *Note: You can use blossoms from zucchini, pumpkin, or other squash varieties. For this recipe, we like cheese curds from the Lone Grazer Creamery and Wagon Party beer from Bauhaus Brew Labs, both widely available in markets around the greater Minneapolis area. To add a little kick, include a slice of pickled jalepeño among the cheese curds.*

1½ cups cooked garbanzo
    beans, rinsed and drained

¼ cup sesame tahini

6 tablespoons extra virgin olive oil

3 cloves garlic

½ cup roasted, peeled,
    and diced red beets

¼ cup fresh lemon juice

1½ teaspoons sea salt

1½ teaspoons pepper

½ cup extra virgin olive oil

Makes 2 cups

Beet Hummus

WISE ACRE EATERY, MINNEAPOLIS   ❧   CHEF BETH FISHER

Wise Acre gets much of its food fresh from its own farm, so the menu changes with the seasons. This vivid dip is an homage to garden-fresh beets. Why not serve it with even more fresh vegetables?

In a small saucepan, heat the garbanzo beans, tahini, and 6 table-spoons of olive oil for 8 to 10 minutes, being careful not to scorch, stirring occasionally.

Meanwhile, puree the garlic, beets, lemon juice, salt, pepper, and ½ cup of olive oil in a blender. Add the blender mixture to the warm pot of beans and tahini and stir together well. Return the mixture to the blender in smaller batches and blend until smooth. Taste and adjust seasonings as you like. Serve with pita and fresh veggies.

Braised Pork Belly

TONGUE IN CHEEK, ST. PAUL & CHEF LEONARD ANDERSON

Soulful foods are best when not rushed. Cook these lip-smacking morsels low and slow, which is best done the day before serving them. Chef Anderson likes to pair these bites with Surly Hell lager.

Preheat the oven to 500 degrees.

Score the fat side of the pork belly in a diamond pattern, cutting only through the top layer of fat, about ¼ to ½ inch. In a small bowl, mix the salt, sugar, and spices together and rub the spice mixture all over the pork belly. Place in a baking dish and roast fat side up for 5 minutes. Turn the heat down to 250 degrees and roast uncovered until a toothpick inserted comes out clean with little resistance, 4 to 5 hours.

Let the pork belly cool in its own fat overnight in the refrigerator. Once the meat has cooled, cut it into bite-size pieces. Heat the oil in a deep fryer or 3-quart saucepan to 350 degrees. Fry the pork belly pieces until crispy, about 2 minutes. Serve with fruit salsas, chutneys, pickles, or just on its own.

3 pounds skinless pork belly

1 tablespoon salt

3 tablespoons brown sugar

1 tablespoon ground ginger

1 teaspoon crushed red
   pepper flakes

1 teaspoon pepper

4 cups soybean oil
   or other high-heat
   oil for frying

Makes 15 small bites

1 tablespoon canola oil

1 shallot, peeled and thinly sliced

2 cups chanterelle mushrooms,
cleaned and trimmed
to equal sizes

2 bay leaves

½ cup white wine vinegar

1 cup extra virgin olive oil

3 sprigs fresh thyme

Salt and pepper

Makes 2 cups

Chanterelles à la Greque

CORNER TABLE, MINNEAPOLIS CHEF THOMAS BOEMER

Wild chanterelles can be found growing in the woods in Minnesota in late summer and early fall depending on the part of the state you explore. Preserve them packed in a vinaigrette and include them in a charcuterie tray with crusty bread.

Heat the canola oil in a large sauté pan over medium heat and add the sliced shallots. Cook for a few minutes until translucent. Increase the heat and add the chanterelles; cook for 3 to 4 minutes. Add the bay leaves, white wine vinegar, olive oil, and thyme sprigs and remove from heat. Let the chanterelles sit in the pan and steep for 10 to 15 minutes. Taste and adjust the seasonings with salt and pepper.

Cool to room temperature, transfer to a jar, seal with a lid, and store in the refrigerator. Serve with crusty bread, cheeses, olives, and cured meats.

Fermented Herb Yogurt Dip

GYST FERMENTATION BAR, MINNEAPOLIS
CO-OWNER AND CHEF MELANIE GUSE

Fermenting the herbs before stirring them into this creamy dip adds a depth of flavor you don't get from quickly mixed in fresh herbs. If you've wanted to experiment with fermentation, this recipe is a great way to begin.

Place the chopped herbs, chile, and garlic in a 1-quart mason jar. Dissolve the salt in the warm water and pour the brine over the herbs in the mason jar. Place plastic wrap on top of the herbs and weigh this down with the lid from a smaller jar topped with pie weights sealed in a plastic bag, so the herbs are completely submerged under the brine. Cover the jar loosely with a canning jar lid. Let the jar sit for 1 week at room temperature in a cool, dark place.

After a week, drain the water from the fermented herbs. In a small bowl, mix the herbs into the yogurt and add the lemon juice. In a small pan, heat the minced shallot with a splash of vegetable oil and caramelize until golden. Let cool and add the shallot to the yogurt mixture. Refrigerate the dip for at least 2 hours before serving. Serve with potato chips or your favorite fresh-cut veggies. This dip keeps well for at least 1 week.

1 small bunch fresh dill,
    finely chopped

1 small bunch fresh chives,
    finely chopped

1 dry hot red chile, such as
    a Thai chile or chile de árbol,
    finely chopped

2 cloves garlic, finely chopped

2 tablespoons salt

1 quart warm water

24 ounces whole-milk Greek yogurt

1 lemon, juiced

1 small shallot, minced

Makes 3½ cups

Fried green tomatoes

4 cups sunflower oil for frying

4 large (baseball size) firm
    green tomatoes

2 cups flour

2 tablespoons sea salt

1 tablespoon black pepper

1 teaspoon cayenne pepper

6 eggs, beaten

3 cups cornmeal

Skillet sweet corn vinaigrette

½ pound (5 to 6 slices) bacon,
    rough chopped

2 tablespoons bacon fat,
    reserved from cooking bacon

2 cups diced yellow onion

2 cups sweet corn, cut off the cob

1 cup apple cider vinegar

½ cup extra virgin olive oil

1 tablespoon coarse ground mustard

2 tablespoons honey

1 cup mixed herbs (chives, basil,
    tarragon), rough chopped

1 tablespoon salt

2 teaspoons pepper

Serves 4 to 6

Fried Green Tomatoes with Skillet Sweet Corn Vinaigrette

WISE ACRE EATERY, MINNEAPOLIS   ❧   CHEF BETH FISHER

Summers are short but glorious in Minnesota. When the air turns cool and you still have tomatoes unripened on the vine, you'll want to make this recipe for a "last hurrah" of the season.

For the fried green tomatoes:
Heat the sunflower oil in a 3-quart saucepan over medium heat while you prepare the tomatoes and dredging mixture.

Slice the tomatoes ½ inch thick. Mix the flour, salt, black pepper, and cayenne pepper in a pie plate. Whisk the eggs together in a small bowl. Put the cornmeal in another pie plate or shallow bowl. Take the tomato slices, one at a time, and dredge in the flour mixture, then the beaten egg, and then the cornmeal to coat evenly. Set the coated tomato slices on a sheet pan as you work.

Line another baking sheet with parchment.

When all the tomato slices are ready, turn the heat to medium-high for the pan with the sunflower oil and check the temperature with a kitchen thermometer. When the oil reaches 350 degrees, carefully slip three or four tomato slices into the oil at one time and fry until golden brown, 3 to 5 minutes. Remove and place the tomato slices on the paper-lined baking sheet. Repeat until all the tomato slices have been fried. Keep warm in the oven at 250 degrees.

(continued on page 30)

For the skillet sweet corn vinaigrette:
Cook the bacon in a large skillet until crispy. Remove the bacon to a plate lined with a paper towel and pour off all but 2 tablespoons of the bacon fat. Heat the bacon fat over medium heat and add the onion. Cook until the onion softens, 3 to 5 minutes. Remove the skillet from the heat and stir in the corn, apple cider vinegar, olive oil, mustard, honey, mixed herbs, salt, and pepper. Spoon over the fried green tomatoes and serve immediately.

8 tablespoons butter, divided

1 cup diced yellow onion

2 tablespoons minced shallot

2 to 3 cloves garlic, smashed
    with the side of a chef's knife

1 cup sliced mushrooms

1 teaspoon fresh thyme leaves

Salt and pepper to taste

1 pound chicken livers, cleaned
    (from True Cost Farm)

¼ cup sherry

1 tablespoon red wine vinegar

Makes about 3 cups

"Gotta Have It" Chicken Liver Pâté

TRUE COST FARM, MONTROSE
OWNERS JACK AND BETSY MCCANN

True Cost Farm provides meat and eggs that are sustainably and locally produced in a CSA model where you build your own package. Liver, a "traditional food," is very nourishing, yet does not have a presence in most modern households. If you have never given liver a chance, this is a great way to try it.

In a large, heavy skillet, melt 4 tablespoons of the butter, add the onions and shallots, and cook over low heat until browned and caramelized. When they are deep golden brown, add the garlic, mushrooms, and thyme and cook until the mushrooms are tender. Add the salt and pepper and transfer to a food processor.

Add the remaining 4 tablespoons of butter to the sauté pan and add the livers when the pan is hot but not smoking. Sear the livers on all sides, turning as needed. Season with salt and pepper. Cook the livers until they are medium rare, not cooked all the way through. This is important—overcooking liver ruins the flavor. Stir in the sherry and red wine vinegar. Remove from heat and let cool.

Once the liver is cool, add it to the food processor. Process until smooth.

Serve with crusty bread. Store in the refrigerator and eat within a week.

½ large yellow onion, sliced thin
(about 1 cup)

5 to 6 cucumbers, sliced,
skin on (about 6 cups)

1½ cups sugar

1½ cups white vinegar

2½ tablespoons kosher salt

½ teaspoon celery seed

1 teaspoon yellow mustard seeds

½ teaspoon turmeric

Makes about 6 cups

Lola Refrigerator Pickles

LOLA—AN AMERICAN BISTRO, NEW ULM
CHEF AND OWNER LACEY LUETH

When your garden is exploding with summer cucumbers, this recipe is a quick and carefree way to make them last. At Lola, they make fifty pounds at a time and serve them with all their sandwiches. These pretty pickles are perfect picnic partners! Say that three times fast!

Place the sliced onions and cucumbers in a heat-proof glass container, bowl, or canning jar. In a saucepan over medium heat, stir together the sugar, vinegar, salt, celery and mustard seeds, and turmeric. Bring to a simmer while stirring to dissolve the sugar.

Remove the brine from the heat and pour over the cucumbers and onions. Refrigerate overnight before serving.

(see photograph on page 21)

Basil pesto

¼ cup walnuts

2 cloves garlic, peeled

⅓ cup shaved Parmesan cheese

2 ounces fresh basil leaves

2 ounces fresh spinach

¾ cup garlic-infused olive oil

2 teaspoons kosher salt

Sun-dried tomato jam

1 head garlic

1 teaspoon olive oil

1 small red bell pepper

½ pound sun-dried tomatoes

¼ cup sambal oelek
     (Thai chile garlic paste)

2 teaspoon kosher salt

2 tablespoons honey

¾ cup extra virgin olive oil

Smoked tomato coulis

1 to 2 cups wood chips
     (hickory or apple)

1 pound tomatoes

Prairie Bay's BYOB (Build Your Own Bruschetta)

PRAIRIE BAY GRILL, BAXTER   ❧   CHEF MATT ANNAND

Chef Annand, a Brainerd native, understands long winters and the desire for fresh flavors harvested right from the garden. Bruschetta makes the perfect palette. This do-it-yourself appetizer is a carefree way to entertain and let guests "wear the chef's hat" while they create their own flavor combinations.

Important: To prepare all the elements for this dish, you will roast a total of four garlic heads and two red bell peppers, and you will grill 1 pound of tomatoes and one or two portobello mushroom caps. Plan ahead to do all the roasting at once; likewise the grilling.

For the basil pesto:
Preheat the oven to 350 degrees. Place the walnuts on a small baking sheet and bake until they just begin to darken and smell toasty, 6 to 8 minutes. Toss the walnuts, garlic, Parmesan cheese, basil, spinach, olive oil, and salt into a food processor or blender and blend until smooth. Adjust seasonings to taste. Cover and refrigerate until ready to serve.

For the sun-dried tomato jam:
Preheat the oven to 400 degrees. Slice the top off the head of garlic to reveal a little of the cloves inside. Place on a square of aluminum foil, drizzle olive oil onto the garlic, and wrap the foil around to seal the head. (At the same time, roast a second garlic head for the smoked tomato coulis recipe below.) Cut the red bell pepper in half and scoop out the seeds. Place the pepper halves and wrapped garlic head on a small baking sheet and roast until the peppers are charred and the garlic is lightly browned and tender, about 30 minutes.

While the garlic and pepper are roasting, bring a medium pot of water to a boil and add the sun-dried tomatoes. Boil for 20 minutes, then drain, reserving 1 cup of the liquid.

¼ cup garlic-infused olive oil

½ medium onion, diced

1 head garlic

¾ cup white wine

¾ cup reserved liquid
    from smoked tomatoes

2 teaspoons kosher salt

1 cup olive oil

Bread and toppings

1 red bell pepper, roasted,
    seeded and peeled,
    and cut into strips

1 to 2 portobello mushroom caps,
    marinated and grilled, sliced

2 heads roasted garlic

1 yellow onion, julienned,
    deeply caramelized in
    2 tablespoons butter

4 ounces fresh mozzarella, sliced
    (at Prairie Bay they smoke
    it over cherry wood)

1 baguette

Balsamic vinegar reduction
    and flavorful extra virgin
    olive oil for drizzling

12 fresh basil leaves, whole,
    removed from stem

2 ounces Parmesan cheese,
    shaved into thin strips
    with a vegetable peeler

Serves 4 to 6 with extra spreads
for another BYOB gathering

Let the roasted garlic and red bell pepper cool. Squeeze the garlic cloves out of their skin and peel the skin off the pepper halves.

Add the garlic, red bell pepper, sun-dried tomatoes, sambal oelek, salt, and honey to the bowl of a food processor and blend until smooth. Add the reserved liquid from the sun-dried tomatoes as needed. Slowly drizzle in the olive oil while the food processor is running to emulsify. Cover and refrigerate until ready to serve.

For the smoked tomato coulis:
Soak the wood chips in water for 30 minutes, then drain. Heat one side of the smoker or grill, leaving the other side with no direct heat. When the temperature reaches 250 degrees, add the wood chips. Slice the tomatoes, spread them on metal pie tins, and place on the unheated side of the grill. Cover and smoke for 15 to 20 minutes. Remove to cool. Reserve ¾ cup of the juice from the smoked tomatoes.

In a large saucepan, heat the garlic-infused olive oil over medium heat, add the onion, and sauté until golden brown. Add the roasted garlic (see steps under sun-dried tomato jam). Deglaze with the white wine and simmer until almost completely reduced. Add the smoked tomatoes, reserved smoked tomato juice, and salt and simmer for 10 minutes. Transfer the tomato mixture to a blender and blend while slowly drizzling in the olive oil. Cover and refrigerate until ready to serve.

For the bread and toppings:
To serve, arrange all the elements in appropriate bowls and dishes and let guests create their own bruschetta.

Smoked trout

¾ pound smoked trout (or salmon), ¼-inch dice

⅓ cup crème fraîche

¼ lemon, juiced

1 tablespoon capers

1 tablespoon finely diced red onions

2 sprigs parsley, finely chopped

Kosher salt to taste

Buttered toast

4 slices Pain de Mie bread

2 tablespoons butter, melted

Scrambled eggs

4 eggs, lightly beaten

1 tablespoon plus 1 teaspoon heavy cream

2 teaspoons butter

½ teaspoon salt

8 chive spears, thinly sliced

2 tablespoons Lake Superior herring roe

Serves 4

Smoked Trout, Scrambled Eggs, Capers, and Trout Roe on Buttered Toast

THE BACHELOR FARMER, MINNEAPOLIS ❧ CHEF PAUL BERGLUND

The combination of smoked trout, rich crème fraîche, and buttery toast are nice starters in bite-size form, but this dish could easily become an elegant, complete lunch with the addition of fresh salad greens.

For the smoked trout:
In a medium bowl, mix together the trout, crème fraîche, lemon juice, capers, red onions, and parsley. Add salt to taste. Cover and refrigerate.

For the buttered toast:
Use a sharp knife to remove the crust from the bread, and then brush both sides with the melted butter. In a skillet over medium heat, brown the bread two at a time, turning to brown both sides. This should take about 1 minute for each side. Remove the toast and keep warm.

For the scrambled eggs:
Fill a medium saucepan with 1 inch of water and bring to a simmer. Combine the eggs, cream, butter, and salt in a metal bowl that is big enough to set on top of the simmering water. Place the bowl over the saucepan and continuously stir the eggs with a spatula until they are just set and no longer runny. Sprinkle in the chives and remove from heat.

To assemble:
Place one slice of toast on each of four plates. Divide the trout mixture between the four toasts, spreading it to make an even platform for the eggs. Top the trout with the scrambled eggs and then top with the roe. Serve immediately.

1⅔ cups water

2 red onions, thinly sliced

1 carrot, peeled and thinly sliced

2 ribs celery, thinly sliced

5 cloves garlic, thinly sliced

2⅓ cups distilled vinegar

⅔ cup sugar

4 tablespoons kosher salt

1 tablespoon whole allspice

2 bay leaves

½ cup flour

1 teaspoon salt

2 pounds Lake Superior
    herring fillets

3 tablespoons grape seed oil

Serves 10

Soused Herring

THE BACHELOR FARMER, MINNEAPOLIS   ❧   CHEF PAUL BERGLUND

Lake Superior herring, also called lake cisco, has flavor attributes similar to the ocean fish of the same name. Marinating the fish in a briny vegetable vinegar overnight allows the flavors to develop. This process works well with other small fish such as mackerel, sardines, or trout and is a perfect part of a summer smorgasbord.

In a medium-size saucepan, bring the water, sliced vegetables, vinegar, sugar, kosher salt, and spices to a boil. Reduce heat and simmer until the vegetables soften slightly, about 15 minutes. Set aside in a warm place on the stove top.

Place the flour in a baking pan. Salt the fish fillets and then dredge them in the flour, shaking well to remove excess. Heat a large, heavy-bottomed skillet over medium heat and add the grape seed oil. When the pan is very hot but not smoking, add the fish fillets and cook until golden brown on one side, about 3 minutes. Turn and cook another 3 minutes on the other side.

While the fish is cooking, use one-third of the pickled vegetable mixture to form an even layer in a small baking dish that will fit the fish snugly. When the fish is finished cooking, remove the fillets from the pan and shake off excess oil, then arrange half the fillets on top of the pickled vegetables. Cover this fish layer with another third of the pickling mixture. Add the final layer of fish and then top with the remaining pickled vegetables and pickling liquid. Cover and refrigerate, marinating at least 8 hours or overnight before serving.

Serve with hearty wheat or rye bread, crème fraîche, spicy Dijon mustard, and sprigs of fresh dill.

Curried fish cakes

1 pound walleye fillets,
    skin and bones removed

4 tablespoons Thai red curry paste

1 egg

8 kaffir (makrut) lime leaves,
    thinly sliced

1 cup fresh green beans, thinly sliced

½ teaspoon salt

3 cups oil for frying

Cucumber salad

2 medium cucumbers, peeled,
    seeded, quartered lengthwise,
    and thinly sliced

1 shallot, thinly sliced

½ cup white vinegar

½ cup sugar

½ teaspoon salt

¼ cup finely chopped peanuts

Cilantro leaves, for garnish

Serves 4 to 6

Tod Mun Pla: Curried Fish Cakes with Cucumber Salad

SEN YAI SEN LEK, NORTHEAST MINNEAPOLIS
CHEF JOE HATCH-SURISOOK

Aromatic Thai flavors take walleye—an essential Minnesota white fish—on a journey to Southeast Asia. Chef Hatch-Surisook brings his native Thai cuisine to the Northeast Minneapolis community and incorporates many local foods into his menu.

For the curried fish cakes:
Puree the fillets in a food processor or blender until processed to a smooth, mousse-like consistency. Transfer to a mixing bowl. Add the curry paste, egg, lime leaves, green beans, and salt and mix well.

Spray a cookie sheet with nonstick spray. Fill a bowl with water to dip your hands in while shaping the mixture into patties. Dip your hands in the water bowl and then scoop a scant ¼-cup measure of the fish mixture. Shape it into a patty about 2 inches round and ½ inch thick and set aside on the greased cookie sheet. Repeat with the remaining fish mixture, making about twelve patties, and refrigerate the tray of patties.

For the cucumber salad:
Place the cucumbers and shallots in a medium bowl. In a small bowl, whisk together the vinegar, sugar, and salt and pour over the cucumbers and shallots. Set aside to marinate while you fry the fish cakes.

To assemble:
In a heavy saucepan, heat the oil to 325 degrees. Fry each fish cake until golden brown, carefully turning over to cook both sides evenly. Remove the fried cakes with a slotted spatula and drain on paper towels. Sprinkle chopped peanuts over the cucumber salad and plate with the hot fish cakes. Scatter with cilantro leaves as a garnish.

16 ounces Boundary Waters
    Brunette Brown Ale

1 cup heavy cream

1 teaspoon olive oil

½ yellow onion, minced

2 cloves garlic, minced

Pinch salt

3 ounces white queso, grated

2 ounces white Cheddar, grated

2 ounces yellow Cheddar, grated

Serves 6 to 8

Voyageur Brewing
Beer Cheese Fondue

VOYAGEUR BREWING COMPANY, GRAND MARAIS
CHEF CHARLES CONROY

Here in Minnesota we love our beer . . . and cheese! The Boundary Waters Brunette Brown Ale in this recipe is made with Minnesota-grown wild rice. At the taproom, they serve this luscious fondue with sautéed Brussels sprouts, apple slices, and their house-made sourdough bread.

In separate saucepans, heat the beer and the cream and simmer until they are each reduced by half their original volume. While the liquids are reducing, heat the olive oil in a small sauté pan. Add the onions and garlic with a pinch of salt and sauté until caramelized. When the beer and cream are reduced by half, combine them in one saucepan and add the onions and garlic. Slowly stir in the grated queso and white Cheddar and reduce the heat to low, stirring until smooth. Add the grated yellow Cheddar just before serving.

Serve warm with cubes of sourdough bread, sliced apples, or Bacon–Glazed Brussels Sprouts *(see the recipe in the Salads and Sides section, page 42).*

Salads & Sides

Buttered Popcorn Gnocchi with Port Wine Reduction, p. 44

1 pound Brussels sprouts, trimmed

3 slices thick-cut bacon

1 cup finely chopped onion

8 cloves garlic, sliced

⅓ cup sugar

⅓ cup water

2½ teaspoons tamari

2½ teaspoons Worcestershire sauce

2½ tablespoons sherry vinegar

Pinch sea salt

Pinch crushed chili flakes

1 tablespoon canola or sunflower oil

2 tablespoons chilled butter

Serves 6 as a side dish
or 8 as an appetizer

Bacon-Glazed Brussels Sprouts

ICEHOUSE, MINNEAPOLIS   ❧   CHEF MATT BICKFORD

Icehouse has it all: great food and cocktails, a cool atmosphere, and live music. The "small plates" they serve are perfect for nibbling with drinks. Serve these tasty morsels as a side dish or as a bar nosh. At Icehouse, Chef Bickford smokes the onions and garlic for added flavor.

Bring a large pot of water to a boil. Cut an "X" in the stem end of each Brussels sprout to allow for even cooking. Blanch the Brussels sprouts for 3 to 5 minutes in the boiling water. Drain them and chill immediately by plunging into ice water, draining, and spreading onto a baking sheet. Refrigerate for 1 hour. When the Brussels sprouts are cooled, cut in half lengthwise.

Cut the bacon into ¼-inch pieces. Place the bacon in a cold cast-iron skillet and heat over medium heat, stirring occasionally to evenly crisp the bacon. Remove the bacon pieces and drain on parchment paper. Leave the bacon fat in the pan and reduce heat to medium-low.

Add the onions and garlic to the bacon fat and cook, stirring occasionally, until caramelized, 20 to 25 minutes.

Meanwhile, stir the sugar and water together in a sauté pan over medium heat. Simmer until most of the water has evaporated, forming a thick syrup. When the onions are caramelized, add them to the sugar syrup and stir to coat. Add the tamari, Worcestershire sauce, vinegar, salt, and chili flakes and stir while simmering until it forms a thick, syrupy consistency, 20 to 30 minutes.

Heat the oil in a large, heavy skillet. Add the Brussels sprouts, cut side down, and sear until they are well browned. Deglaze with the dressing and stir to coat. Simmer for a few minutes to heat through and swirl in the chilled butter, stirring just until incorporated. Toss in the reserved bacon pieces before serving.

❧ ***Note:*** *The sugar syrup dressing can be prepared a day or two in advance and refrigerated until you're ready to cook the Brussels sprouts.*

Burdock Mashed Potatoes

SALT CELLAR, ST. PAUL   &   CHEF ALAN BERGO

Here is a perfect example of Chef Bergo's use of local and obscure ingredients prepared with simple, classic technique. He dreamed up this dish when faced with piles of burdock root. Alan cooked it like a European might—with cream—and found it to have a sweet, almost oyster-y quality. Look for burdock root at local food co-ops or Asian markets.

2 cups heavy cream

6 ounces burdock root

2 pounds russet potatoes

2 tablespoons butter

Salt and white pepper to taste

Serves 6 to 8

Pour the cream into a 1½-quart saucepan. Peel the burdock roots and chop, immediately adding them to the cream to prevent oxidization. When all the roots are chopped and in the pot, bring the mixture to a simmer and cook on low heat until the burdock is tender, about 45 minutes.

Pour the burdock cream into a blender and puree until smooth, adding a little water if needed to thin the mixture. Pass the burdock cream through a fine strainer and reserve.

Heat a large pot of lightly salted water. Peel the potatoes and add them whole to the pot. Cook until tender, about 15 minutes. Remove the potatoes from the water and rice them with a potato ricer into a large bowl. Add the burdock cream and butter and stir well to combine. Season with salt and pepper to taste.

Buttered popcorn gnocchi

½ cup popcorn kernels
(Chef Beran prefers
Clem's Homegrown)

9 tablespoons butter, divided

½ cup semolina flour

½ tablespoon salt

1 teaspoon pepper

2 teaspoons smoked hot
Spanish paprika

1 egg

1 cup flour

Port wine reduction

1 ½ cups port wine

½ cup sugar

1 star anise

2 bay leaves

2 sprigs fresh thyme

Presentation

3 tablespoons butter

1 cup mâche (lamb's lettuce)
or arugula greens

¼ pound smoked Cheddar cheese

Serves 4 as an entrée
or 6 as a side dish

Buttered Popcorn Gnocchi with Port Wine Reduction

LAKE AVENUE RESTAURANT, DULUTH   CHEF TONY BERAN

The very thought of a mash-up between buttered popcorn and gnocchi will make you go "Mmmmm." At Lake Avenue, they serve this dish as a side for pickled pork tongue, but it also pairs well with sausages, grilled meats, and fish.

For the buttered popcorn gnocchi:
In a large pot over medium heat, combine the popcorn kernels with 2 tablespoons of the melted butter. Cover and cook, shaking vigorously until all the kernels have popped.

In another large pot, bring 8 cups of water to a boil. Add 4 table-spoons of the butter. Once the butter has melted, pour the popped popcorn into the boiling water and simmer for 2 minutes. Strain the buttered popcorn water back into a pot for cooking the gnocchi later. Run the blanched popcorn through a food mill and discard the hulls. In a medium bowl, mix the strained popcorn pulp with the semolina, salt, pepper, and paprika.

Melt 3 tablespoons of the butter and, in a separate bowl, beat the butter with the egg. Add the popcorn mixture and the egg mixture to a food processor and blend until well combined. Add the flour and blend until smooth. Place the dough into a piping bag fitted with a ¼-inch tip or into a resealable plastic bag with a ¼-inch hole cut from one corner. Bring the buttered popcorn water back to a boil. Pipe the dough into the water, cutting it with scissors at ⅜-inch intervals. Once the gnocchi float, let them cook for 1 more minute and then remove with a slotted spoon and spread onto a parchment-lined baking sheet. Allow to cool.

For the port wine reduction:
In a small saucepan over medium heat, combine the port, sugar, star anise, bay leaves, and thyme sprigs. Simmer until reduced by half. Strain and reserve the liquid.

For the presentation:
Brown the 3 tablespoons of butter in a nonstick skillet. Add the gnocchi and let them sit untouched for 1 minute to brown. Toss the gnocchi in the pan to brown on all sides and then divide onto plates. Drizzle each serving with the port reduction and garnish with greens. Grate the smoked Cheddar over each plate to finish. Serve immediately.

Carrot-Family Slaw with Dill and Cilantro

THE NEW MIDWESTERN TABLE, PARK RAPIDS   ❧   AMY THIELEN

The aromatic qualities of the carrot family (of the family Apiaceae) shine in this simple salad that celebrates a bounty from the garden. Practice your knife skills and julienne the carrots (see Note), or use a food processor fitted with a coarse grater disc. This slaw makes a great side dish for poultry or seafood.

Put the cumin seeds on a cutting board, cover with a drop of oil, and mince finely. In a medium bowl, mix together the cumin, carrots, salt, sugar (if needed), ground coriander seed, pepper flakes, cilantro, dill, and olive oil. Marinate in the refrigerator for at least 3 hours before serving.

❧ **Note:** *For large carrots, use a julienne peeler, available at most kitchen stores. Fresh garden carrots may be too slender for the peeler. Chef Thielen uses a technique she learned from Chinese chefs. Peel the carrots. Then, starting at the fat end, slice them into thin, long coins, on a deep diagonal. Work neatly so that the coins stay in a stacked line. With the knife upright, thinly slice the coins, making thin, even strips. If you keep things neat on the cutting board, this goes quickly, faster than you can say "mandoline."*

½ teaspoon cumin seeds

1 drop olive oil

8 cups (2 pounds) julienned carrots

¾ teaspoon salt

1 teaspoon sugar (if the carrots aren't garden-sweet)

1 teaspoon ground coriander seed

¼ teaspoon pepper flakes

3 tablespoons chopped cilantro

3 tablespoons chopped dill

1 tablespoon extra virgin olive oil

Serves 6 to 8

3 cloves garlic, whole and unpeeled

¼ cup buttermilk

2 tablespoons minced fresh parsley

2 tablespoons minced fresh chives

1 tablespoon minced fresh tarragon

1 tablespoon minced fresh cilantro

½ tablespoon minced fresh dill

½ teaspoon Worcestershire sauce

1 teaspoon salt

½ lemon, zested and juiced

1 cup Greek yogurt

Makes 1½ cups

Green Goddess Dressing

ICEHOUSE, MINNEAPOLIS   ❧   CHEF MATT BICKFORD

Like a walk through an herb garden, this verdant dressing gives a lift to fresh salad greens and works as a dip for veggies too. Whip up a batch when gardens and farmers' markets offer abundant produce.

Preheat the oven to 350 degrees.

Place the garlic cloves in a small baking dish or ramekin and cover with foil. Roast the garlic until softened, 10 to 15 minutes. Allow the garlic to cool before squeezing the softened roasted garlic from the skin. Discard the garlic skin and add the garlic to a blender along with the buttermilk, herbs, Worcestershire sauce, and salt. Blend until smooth, stirring down sides with a spatula to blend completely. Whisk in the lemon zest, juice, and yogurt.

Refrigerate until ready to serve. This dip keeps well refrigerated for a week or more.

Slaw

2 cups fresh green, wax, romano, or other heirloom beans

1 tablespoon olive oil

Salt and pepper to taste

2 cups shredded green cabbage

¼ cup chopped fresh parsley

¼ cup chopped fresh chives

Dressing

1 tablespoon champagne vinegar

1 teaspoon Dijon mustard

1 teaspoon coarsely chopped shallots

¼ teaspoon Tabasco sauce

¼ cup olive oil

1 teaspoon celery seeds

¼ cup mayonnaise

Salt and pepper to taste

Makes 4 cups of slaw

Grilled Bean Slaw

LUCIA'S RESTAURANT, MINNEAPOLIS   ❧   CHEF RYAN LUND

Grilling garden-fresh green beans gives this slaw a smokiness while still maintaining the color and crunch of the beans. Try a pretty variety of heirloom beans and look for unique types like Dragon Tongue or Rattlesnake.

For the slaw:
In a medium bowl, toss the beans in the olive oil and season with salt and pepper. Grill over high heat until lightly charred. Place in a large bowl and allow to cool. When beans have cooled, add the shredded cabbage, parsley, and chives.

For the dressing:
In a blender, mix the vinegar, mustard, shallots, Tabasco sauce, and olive oil until smooth. Stir in the celery seeds and mayonnaise and add salt and pepper to taste.

Toss the vegetables with the dressing and serve immediately.

2 tablespoons fish sauce

2 tablespoons minced lemongrass

1 teaspoon sugar

4 ounces fresh mixed salad greens

2 tomatoes, cut into wedges

2 tablespoons vegetable oil

3 cloves garlic, minced

1 pound pork tenderloin,
    thinly sliced

1 medium yellow onion,
    thinly sliced

Serves 2 to 4

Lemongrass Pork Tenderloin over Mixed Greens

RAINBOW CHINESE RESTAURANT, MINNEAPOLIS
CHEF AND OWNER TAMMY WONG

You may run into Chef Wong at the Minneapolis farmers' market where she teaches a cooking class and shops for the freshest produce for her restaurant. "Fresh greens, garlic, and onions stir-fried over a searing flame—those are the basic elements of what I do," she says.

In a small bowl, mix the fish sauce, lemongrass, and sugar. Arrange the mixed greens and tomato wedges on a serving platter.

Heat the oil in a wok or large sauté pan over high heat. Add the garlic and sauté until slightly browned. Add the pork and stir constantly, until pork is just cooked through. Add the lemongrass mixture and onions to the pan. Cook for 2 to 3 minutes, stirring constantly. Dish the pork over the mixed greens and tomatoes and serve immediately.

Minnesota "nice-oise" salad

6 medium potatoes

1 red onion

1 bunch garlic scapes

1 bunch asparagus, trimmed

2 tablespoons olive oil

Salt and pepper to taste

12-ounce salmon fillet

1 pound salad greens or spinach

4 eggs, hard cooked and peeled, cut in half

1 cup capers, drained

¼ cup basil leaves, chopped

Dressing

¼ cup maple syrup

¼ cup Dijon mustard

¼ cup lemon juice

6 cloves garlic, minced

⅓ cup olive oil

Salt and pepper to taste

Serves 6

Minnesota "Nice-oise" Salad with Salmon

GOOD LIFE CATERING, MINNEAPOLIS
CHEF AND CO-OWNER JENNY BREEN

A Minnesotan will leave the last slice of cake on the platter for someone else, even if they really wanted it . . . you know, to be "Minnesota Nice." They may grumble when someone else finally eats the cake, but only under their breath. Whatever Minnesota nice may mean to you, this salad offers an abundance of local flavor and color—and makes enough to invite the neighbors over.

Preheat the grill.

For the Minnesota "nice-oise" salad:
Cut the potatoes into quarters and slice the onion into ½–inch strips. Brush the potatoes, onion, garlic scapes, and asparagus with olive oil and season with salt and pepper. Grill the vegetables until nicely charred, 10 to 12 minutes for the onion, garlic, and asparagus and 20 to 25 minutes for the potatoes.

Brush the salmon with oil and season with salt and pepper. Grill over medium–high heat for about 8 minutes per side. The salmon should be thoroughly cooked but not overcooked or dry. Refrigerate the vegetables and salmon.

For the dressing:
In a small bowl, whisk together the maple syrup, mustard, and lemon juice. Add the minced garlic, olive oil, salt, and pepper and whisk until combined.

Place the salad greens on a large platter and artfully arrange the vegetables, eggs, and salmon over the top of the greens. Sprinkle the salad with capers and basil and drizzle with the dressing.

Açai vinaigrette

1 tablespoon minced fresh
    ginger root

1 tablespoon minced garlic

2 tablespoons minced shallots

1 cup champagne vinegar

1 tablespoon orange juice
    frozen concentrate (not diluted)

⅓ cup brown sugar

½ teaspoon dried thyme

½ teaspoon dried tarragon

1½ tablespoons cream sherry

¾ cup açai juice

1¼ cups grape seed oil
    or canola oil

½ cup fresh raspberries

½ cup fresh blueberries

⅓ cup golden raisins

Raw vegetable salad

3 each breakfast radishes

½ each watermelon radish

6 each baby beets, red, gold,
    and Chioggia

3 each baby heirloom carrots

2 pieces broccolini, tops only,
    cut in half

½ cup fresh blueberries,
    sliced in half

½ cup English shell peas

Salt and pepper to taste

Serves 4 with plenty of leftover dressing

Raw Vegetable Salad with Açai Vinaigrette

NEW SCENIC CAFÉ, DULUTH
CHEF AND OWNER SCOTT GRADEN

It's best to take the scenic route, especially when you are on Scenic Highway 61 between Duluth and Two Harbors. The New Scenic offers a fantastic view, beautiful food, and a garden. This salad is edible art! The dressing recipe makes plenty, which is great to have on hand for other salads.

For the açai vinaigrette:

In a blender, mix together the ginger, garlic, shallots, vinegar, orange juice concentrate, brown sugar, thyme, tarragon, cream sherry, and açai juice until smooth. While the blender is running, slowly drizzle in the oil and blend until emulsified. Turn off the blender and add the raspberries and blueberries. Pulse a few times to blend the berries until the mixture is smooth. Stir in the golden raisins by hand and refrigerate the vinaigrette until ready to use.

For the raw vegetable salad:

Using a mandoline slicer or the slicer plate on a box grater, slice the radishes, beets, and carrots into wafer-thin discs. As you slice each type of root vegetable, place them in separate bowls of ice water to preserve their color and crispness. When all the root vegetables are sliced, arrange them in layers on four salad plates. Drizzle every other layer with 1 to 2 teaspoons of the vinaigrette. Continue layering until all the vegetables are used and then top with the broccolini, blueberries, and peas. Season with salt and pepper and garnish as desired. At the New Scenic, they garnish with edible flowers picked right from their garden.

Roasted Beet Salad with Sherry Pepper Vinaigrette

THE CURIOUS GOAT FOOD TRUCK, MINNEAPOLIS
CHEF IAN GRAY

You probably can't throw an onion in Minneapolis without hitting a restaurant that serves a beet salad, but they are sometimes overly complicated, with busy vinaigrettes and candied nuts. At The Curious Goat, they keep it pure and simple, letting the trio of the beets, chèvre, and arugula shine.

Roasted beet salad

4 to 5 medium beets

3½ cups arugula, washed and loosely packed

8 ounces chèvre (such as Singing Hills Goat Dairy Chèvre)

Sherry pepper vinaigrette

¼ cup sherry vinegar

1 tablespoon hot sauce of your choice

1 tablespoon minced garlic

½ cup extra virgin olive oil

Salt and pepper to taste

Serves 4 to 6

Preheat the oven to 350 degrees.

For the roasted beet salad:
Rinse the beets, place them in a roasting pan with a little water, and cover with aluminum foil. Roast the beets until a fork slides easily into the middle, at least 2 hours. Let cool thoroughly, then rub off the skin and cut into 1-inch cubes.

For the sherry pepper vinaigrette:
In a food processor, blend together the vinegar, hot sauce, and garlic and then slowly drizzle in the olive oil. Add salt and pepper to taste.

Toss the beets and arugula together with the vinaigrette and top with crumbled chèvre.

2 heads cauliflower

2 tablespoons canola oil

2 tablespoons chopped fresh mint

¼ cup golden raisins

2 tablespoons chopped cornichons

½ lemon, juiced

Salt and pepper to taste

¼ cup (2 ounces) shredded
    Parmesan cheese

Serves 4

Roasted Cauliflower with Mint, Golden Raisins, Cornichons, and Parmesan

ZZEST CAFÉ, ROCHESTER   ✺   CHEF JUSTIN SCHOVILLE

Roasted cauliflower has become all the rage, and it seems to be appearing in restaurants everywhere. The unexpected bursts of fresh mint and sweet golden raisins are a piquant addition. At Zzest, they like to get their cauliflower from the Rochester Farmers' Market during the growing season.

Preheat the oven to 425 degrees.

Core the cauliflower heads and cut the florets into bite-size pieces. Pour the canola oil on a sheet pan and heat the pan in the oven for about 5 minutes. The pan should be nice and hot to help the cauliflower brown and also to keep it from sticking to the pan. When the pan is hot, spread the cauliflower in the pan. Roast for 10 minutes and then stir. Continue roasting the cauliflower for another 10 minutes. When the cauliflower is golden brown, place it into a large bowl and add the mint, raisins, cornichons, and lemon juice and season with salt and pepper. Sprinkle Parmesan cheese on top before serving.

16 ramps

1 tablespoon extra virgin olive oil

½ cup shelled pumpkin seeds

4 ounces firm chèvre log

¼ cup pumpkin seed oil

2 tablespoons fresh lemon juice

½ teaspoon coarse salt

1 head red leaf lettuce

1 bunch watercress,
    tough stems removed

½ pint raspberries

Serves 4

Roasted Ramps and Watercress with Pumpkin Seed Chèvre Medallions

COOKBOOK AUTHOR, TEACHER, AND PRIVATE CHEF, MINNEAPOLIS CHEF ROBIN ASBELL

This salad is a poem to spring, with the fresh and vibrant flavors of ramps and watercress accented by tangy chèvre. Roasting the ramps gives them a soulful, subtle flavor.

Preheat the oven to 400 degrees.

Trim and clean the ramps, leaving the green tops intact. In a medium bowl, toss the ramps with olive oil and then place in a roasting pan. Cover the pan tightly with aluminum foil. Roast for 20 minutes, or less if the ramps are thin.

While the ramps are roasting, spread the pumpkin seeds on a small baking sheet and toast in the oven till lightly brown (watch closely so they don't scorch), 5 to 10 minutes.

When the ramps are soft (poke with a paring knife), uncover and set aside to cool.

Chop the pumpkin seeds and spread on a plate. Slice the chilled chèvre log into medallions and roll in the chopped pumpkin seeds to coat.

In a small bowl, whisk the pumpkin seed oil with the lemon juice and salt and set aside.

Wash and dry the lettuce, then tear into pieces. Arrange the lettuce on four plates and top with the watercress and raspberries. Arrange the coated chèvre and four ramps on each plate. Drizzle with the dressing and serve.

2 carrots

2 parsnips

2 turnips

½ to 1 teaspoon Chinese
    five-spice powder

Salt and pepper to taste

¼ teaspoon chili flakes,
    or to taste

¼ cup extra virgin olive oil

¼ cup real Minnesota
    maple syrup

Serves 4 to 6

Roasted Root Vegetables

CAFE LEVAIN, MINNEAPOLIS   ❧   CHEF ADAM VICKERMAN

You can't get any more down-to-earth than root vegetables. The addition of Chinese five-spice powder adds an exotic flavor. These make a nice side dish to Chef Adam Vickerman's recipe for Braised Beef Pot Roast (see the recipe in the Main Courses section, page 88).

Preheat the oven to 325 degrees.

Wash the carrots, parsnips, and turnips and dice with the skin on. (If the parsnips are waxed, peel them before dicing.)

In a large bowl, toss the diced vegetables with the five-spice powder, salt, pepper, chili flakes, olive oil, and maple syrup to coat. Spread on a baking pan and roast until the vegetables are caramelized and tender, 20 to 25 minutes. Serve immediately.

Savory Bread Pudding

HONEY AND RYE BAKEHOUSE, ST. LOUIS PARK
CHEF AND OWNER ANNE ANDRUS

This savory bread pudding takes the idea of traditional bread stuffing to a whole new level. The feel-good addition of greens makes it a righteous accompaniment for any holiday meal when feeding a crowd. You'll crave leftovers; it reheats beautifully for a post-holiday breakfast served with an egg on top.

½ pound ground sausage

3 tablespoons butter

1 clove garlic, minced

⅓ cup diced onion

¼ teaspoon dried sage

¼ teaspoon salt

¼ teaspoon pepper

Pinch crushed red pepper flakes (optional)

2 cups well-packed destemmed spinach, kale, or Swiss chard

1-pound loaf (8 cups) day-old sourdough bread, cubed

1½ cups grated Swiss cheese

3 eggs

1½ cups heavy cream

Serves 8 to 10

Preheat the oven to 375 degrees. Butter an 8-inch square baking dish.

Brown the sausage in a large skillet with the butter, garlic, onion, and spices. In a large bowl, pour the browned sausage over the greens and toss to wilt the greens.

Spread 4 cups of the bread cubes in the buttered baking dish, cover with half of the sausage mixture, and top with ¾ cup of the Swiss cheese. Repeat the layers, finishing with Swiss cheese on top.

Whisk the eggs and cream together to form a custard and pour over the bread, sausage, and cheese layers. Press down to help the custard soak into the bread. Let rest for 10 minutes.

Butter one side of a sheet of aluminum foil and cover the pan. Use a toothpick to poke a few holes in the top. Bake for 30 minutes covered with the foil. Then remove the foil and bake until the cheese is melted and lightly toasted, about 10 additional minutes.

Sofrito

½ yellow onion, chopped

1 green bell pepper, chopped

10 cloves garlic, peeled

½ bunch cilantro, chopped

¼ cup pitted green olives, chopped

1 tablespoon capers

1 ½ teaspoons pepper

1 ½ teaspoons chopped fresh
    oregano

1 teaspoon kosher salt

¼ cup olive oil

2 tablespoons olive oil, for cooking

Potatoes

1 pound Yukon gold (B size) potatoes

Citrus crema

2 cups regular sour cream

½ lime, zested

¼ lime, juiced

Pinch salt

Garnish

⅓ cup pitted, halved kalamata olives

⅓ cup fresh parsley leaves,
    plucked off stem

Serves 4 to 6

Sofrito Potatoes

HOLA AREPA, MINNEAPOLIS
CHEF AND OWNER CHRISTINA NGUYEN

Sofrito is a Latin American "secret weapon" sauce that is simple to prepare and can be used in a variety of recipes to add aromatic flavors. Refrigerated, the sauce keeps well for seven days or may be frozen in small batches. You'll want to keep this sauce on hand for other cooking adventures!

For the sofrito:
Add the onion, bell pepper, garlic, cilantro, green olives, capers, pepper, oregano, and salt to the bowl of a food processor and process until there aren't any big chunks left, but it isn't as smooth as pesto. Stir in the olive oil. This makes about 2 cups of sofrito. Put into a covered container and refrigerate until ready to use.

For the potatoes:
Wash the potatoes and cut into 1-inch chunks. Put the potatoes in a large saucepan or pot, cover with cold water, and bring to a boil over medium-high heat. Cook until fork-tender but not mushy; once the water begins to boil, they should be done. Drain and rinse with cool water to prevent further cooking.

For the citrus crema:
In a medium bowl, stir together the sour cream, lime zest and juice, and salt.

To assemble:
Heat 2 tablespoons of olive oil in a heavy sauté pan over medium heat and add ⅔ cup sofrito. Stir and cook some of the "raw" flavor out of the sofrito for a few minutes. Add the potatoes, stir to coat in the sofrito, and cook for 3 or 4 minutes. Season with a pinch or two of kosher salt to taste.

Serve with the citrus crema, kalamata olive halves, and parsley leaves.

1 cup wild rice

3 cups chicken or vegetable stock

½ cup orzo

½ cup (1 stick) butter

½ cup ramps or wild leeks,
    white part only, sliced

1 teaspoon minced garlic

½ pound asparagus, trimmed,
    cut into ½-inch sections

2 baby green-top carrots, diced

3 cups morel mushrooms, quartered

3 sprigs fresh thyme

¼ cup combined chopped fresh
    rosemary, thyme, and parsley

¼ cup coarsely chopped toasted
    hazelnuts

½ cup cream sherry

½ cup shredded Parmesan cheese

Salt and pepper to taste

Serves 8

Wild Rice Orzotto with Morels, Ramps, and Hazelnuts

WAVES OF SUPERIOR CAFE, TOFTE
CHEF JUDI BARSNESS

Waves of Superior Cafe is located at the Surfside resort on the North Shore. Chef Barsness, formerly of Chez Jude in Grand Marais, honed her signature culinary style—"Minnesine" or Minnesota contemporary cuisine—based on a commitment to the freshest offerings of the Minnesota seasons: organic, locally grown and harvested, wild-caught, and handcrafted ingredients.

Rinse the wild rice in a strainer under cold running water. Place the rice and 2 cups of the chicken or vegetable stock in a large, heavy pot and bring to a boil. Reduce to a simmer and cover with a lid. Cook until the rice kernels puff up, about 45 minutes. Uncover, fluff with a fork, and let simmer another 5 minutes. Drain any excess water.

While the rice is cooking, in a separate pot, bring the remaining cup of stock to a boil and add the orzo. Stirring occasionally, boil until the orzo is tender, about 15 minutes.

Melt the butter in a large skillet and sauté the ramps and garlic until soft and translucent. Add the asparagus, carrots, mushrooms, and herbs and cook over medium heat until the vegetables are tender and juices are absorbed. Stir in the cooked rice, orzo, and toasted hazelnuts. Add the cream sherry and simmer until the sherry is reduced to 1 tablespoon. Stir in the shredded Parmesan cheese and season with salt and pepper to taste.

Serve hot, with additional grated Parmesan cheese if desired.

Wild rice salad

1 cup wild rice

¾ cup peeled and diced celery

⅓ cup dried cranberries

2 teaspoons minced shallots

¼ cup chopped fresh parsley

¾ cup Vegenaise (original flavor)

Pepper and sea salt to taste

Maple-toasted almonds

1 tablespoon coconut oil

2 tablespoons maple syrup

1 cup blanched and
    slivered almonds

1 teaspoon sea salt

Serves 4 to 6

Wild Rice Salad with Maple-Toasted Almonds

GREEN SCENE, WALKER
CHEF AND OWNER ERIN HAEFELE

About as local as you can get, the Green Scene gathers and roasts its own wild rice. Look for the real deal when it comes to wild rice, not the stuff cultivated in California. Maple-glazed almonds add a nice crunch.

For the wild rice salad:
Rinse the rice in a strainer under cold running water. Place the rice and 3 cups of water in a large, heavy pot and bring to a boil. Reduce to a simmer and cover with a lid. Cook until the rice kernels puff up, about 45 minutes. Uncover, fluff with a fork, and let simmer another 5 minutes. Drain any excess water. You should have 3 to 4 cups of cooked rice, depending on the length of the rice grains. Let cool in a large bowl.

When the rice has cooled to room temperature, add the celery, cranberries, shallots, and parsley and mix well. Stir in the Vegenaise to coat, and season to taste with pepper and sea salt.

For the maple-toasted almonds:
Preheat the oven to 350 degrees.

In a small skillet, melt the coconut oil and add the maple syrup. Put the slivered almonds in a bowl, drizzle with the oil and maple syrup mixture, and toss until well coated. Sprinkle with sea salt.

Spread the almonds on a baking sheet and bake until golden brown, 5 to 7 minutes. Allow to cool on a buttered plate.

Sprinkle the almonds on top of the wild rice salad and serve immediately.

Soups & Stews

Lake Superior Trout and Pumpkin Chowder, p. 70

Charred Bell Pepper Soup with Chèvre and Balsamic Vinegar

TERZO, MINNEAPOLIS
EXECUTIVE CHEF THOMAS BRODER

Late summer farmers' markets are busting with garden-fresh vegetables that seem to be most exuberant just before the first frost. Make this soup with peppers ripened by Minnesota sunshine and put it up in the freezer for the long, cold winter.

Charred bell pepper soup

3 pounds red and yellow
    bell peppers

1 pound red onion

4 tablespoons extra virgin olive oil

4 cloves garlic

1 bay leaf

1 cup white wine

1 cup vegetable stock

2 tablespoons balsamic vinegar

Salt and pepper to taste

Garnish

2 tablespoons (1 ounce) pine nuts

1 cup balsamic vinegar

½ cup olive oil

4 ounces fresh chèvre (such as
    from Stickney Hill Dairy)

Serves 4

For the charred bell pepper soup:
Seed and dice the red and yellow peppers into 1-inch pieces. Chop the red onions into 1-inch dice as well.

Heat a heavy medium saucepan over medium-high heat and coat with the olive oil. Add the peppers and onions and stir occasionally until softened. Allow the peppers and onions to char in spots. This should take about 10 minutes. Mince the garlic. Reduce the heat and add the garlic and bay leaf.

Deglaze with the wine, scraping up bits of flavor from the bottom of the pan. Once the wine has reduced slightly, add the stock and simmer until the liquid is reduced by half and the vegetables are tender. Remove from heat and remove the bay leaf. Stir in the balsamic vinegar. Carefully puree in a blender in small batches, then pour the soup through a fine strainer and return to the pot. Season with salt and pepper to taste.

For the garnish:
Preheat the oven to 375 degrees. Spread the pine nuts on a pie pan and bake, stirring occasionally, until an even golden brown, 5 to 10 minutes.

Turn the range fan on high to vent vinegar fumes. In a medium stainless steel pan, bring the balsamic vinegar to a simmer over medium-high heat. Lower the heat to hold at a low simmer until reduced by half. Remove from heat and let cool.

Rewarm the soup to serving temperature and ladle into bowls. Garnish each bowl with crumbled chèvre, toasted pine nuts, and drizzles of olive oil and balsamic vinegar reduction.

Dhal

1 tablespoon black mustard seeds

2 tablespoons ghee or coconut oil

8 curry leaves, or ½ cup cilantro

1 medium onion, chopped

8 cloves garlic, minced

1 tablespoon ground coriander

1 tablespoon ground cumin

1½ teaspoons ground turmeric

2-inch cinnamon stick

1 (13.5-ounce) can coconut milk

6 cups water

3 cups red lentils

½ to 1 teaspoon salt to taste

Coconut sambol

½ cup shredded unsweetened
    coconut

1 lime, zested and juiced

¼ cup minced onion

1 to 2 teaspoons crushed
    red chile flakes

4 curry leaves

¼ teaspoon salt, or to taste

Serves 6 to 8

Curried Red Lentil Dhal

THE CURRY DIVA, MINNEAPOLIS   ❧   CHEF HEATHER JANSZ

Chef Jansz, aka The Curry Diva, uses the tropical flavors and spices of Sri Lanka to warm the hearts of Minnesotans who enjoy her catering, take-out, and pop-up diner meals at Our Kitchen on West 36th Street. This savory dhal is as nourishing to the soul as it is to the body—a great beginning to a meal or completely comforting on its own.

For the dhal:

Heat a 3-quart pot over medium heat and add the black mustard seeds. Shake the mustard seeds gently in the pan until they begin to pop. Once most of the seeds have popped, add the ghee or coconut oil and stir in the curry leaves or cilantro, onions, and garlic and sauté until the onions begin to soften.

While the onions and garlic are cooking, toast the coriander, cumin, and tumeric in a small sauté pan over medium-low heat, stirring frequently, until fragrant. Remove from heat.

Break the cinnamon stick into a few pieces and add to the pot with the onions and garlic, then add the toasted spices. Sauté for 2 to 3 minutes, stirring until the onions and garlic are well coated with spices. Add the coconut milk, water, and lentils, stirring well to keep the lentils from settling to the bottom of the pan. Simmer the dhal until the lentils are tender, at least 20 minutes, stirring vigorously with a whisk to break up the lentils a bit and make the mixture smooth and creamy. Season with salt to taste.

For the coconut sambol:

While the dhal is simmering, place the shredded coconut in a food processor and add the lime zest and juice, onion, crushed red chile flakes, curry leaves, and salt to taste. Process until the coconut is well coated with the seasonings.

Ladel the warm dhal into bowls and serve topped with the coconut sambol.

Green gazpacho

2 cups chunked honeydew melon

2 tablespoons chopped jalapeño pepper

½ cup chopped green bell pepper

½ cup chopped green onions (scallions)

4 tablespoons chopped fresh Italian parsley

1 cup chopped seedless cucumber

2 cups chopped tomatillos (husks removed)

2 cups chopped white onion

4 tablespoons Banyuls or other red wine vinegar

2 teaspoons fine sea salt

1 teaspoon freshly ground white pepper

Chive sour cream

1 cup sour cream

2 tablespoons chopped fresh chives

1 teaspoon sea salt

½ teaspoon freshly ground Tellicherry black pepper

Serves 4

Green Gazpacho with Chive Sour Cream

HEARTLAND RESTAURANT, ST. PAUL   ❧   CHEF LENNY RUSSO

Late summer in Minnesota brings steamy weather and abundant produce. This recipe is a riff on traditional gazpacho and showcases a variety of green fruits and vegetables found at peak ripeness in July and August. This chilled soup is a perfect partner for a glass of dry rosé or a crisp Riesling.

For the green gazpacho:
In a high-speed blender, add the melon, jalapeño, green bell pepper, green onions, parsley, cucumber, tomatillos, and white onion with the vinegar, sea salt, and white pepper. Puree until smooth. Adjust seasonings according to taste with salt and pepper. Refrigerate until ready to serve.

For the chive sour cream:
In a medium bowl, stir together the sour cream, chives, salt, and pepper until well blended.

Divide the soup into chilled bowls and top each with a dollop of the chive sour cream.

1 pound small red or
  fingerling potatoes

4 ears corn on the cob, shucked

1 tablespoon butter, melted

2 tablespoons olive oil, divided

Kosher salt and pepper to taste

¾ cup diced yellow onion

⅛ teaspoon ground cayenne pepper

3 sprigs fresh thyme, destemmed

½ cup white wine

1½ cups half-and-half

1 cup heavy cream

3 tablespoons minced fresh
  chives, for garnish

Serves 6

Grilled Corn and Potato Chowder

BONICELLI KITCHEN, NORTHEAST MINNEAPOLIS
CHEF AND OWNER LAURA BONICELLI

This soup is perfect for early fall "last hurrah" grilling sessions before the weather turns chilly. Grilling the corn and potatoes adds a subtle smoldering flavor to the cream base.

Preheat the grill to medium-high heat.

Place the potatoes in a medium saucepan and cover with 2 inches of water. Bring to a boil and par cook for 2 to 5 minutes so that potatoes are still a bit firm. Remove the potatoes to an ice bath, cool, and then cut into 1-inch cubes.

Soak the shucked corn in cold water for 15 minutes. Dry the corn-cobs, brush with melted butter, and place directly on the grill grates.

Toss the potatoes with 1 tablespoon of the olive oil, salt, and pepper and place in a grill basket on the grill. Turn the corn and potatoes often until the potatoes are cooked through and the corn has turned golden brown, 8 to 10 minutes. Let the corn cool slightly and cut the kernels from the cobs. Puree 1 cup of the corn in a blender or food processor until smooth.

In a large Dutch oven, heat the remaining 1 tablespoon of olive oil over medium heat and add the onion, cayenne, and thyme. Sauté until the onion is translucent, about 5 minutes. Increase the heat to medium-high, add the wine, and scrape the onion bits from the bottom of the pan. Cook to reduce, stirring continuously. Add the pureed corn, whole kernel corn, potatoes, half-and-half, and cream.

Serve hot and garnish with fresh chives.

1 pound trout bones (optional)

4 cups vegetable stock

2 fresh bay leaves (optional, for trout bone stock)

5 tablespoons butter, divided

½ cup peeled and diced carrot

½ cup diced celery

½ cup diced onion

1 cup diced fresh pumpkin

½ cup diced fresh fennel bulb, fronds reserved for garnish

2 tablespoons sliced garlic

1 tablespoon fresh thyme leaves, picked off stem

½ tablespoon chopped fresh sage leaves

3 cups heavy cream

1 (8-ounce) lake trout fillet, skinned and pin bones removed

Salt and pepper to taste

Serves 6 to 8

Lake Superior Trout and Pumpkin Chowder

LAKE AVENUE RESTAURANT, DULUTH   ❧   CHEF TONY BERAN

Canal Park has undergone many dramatic changes since the canal was built in the 1870s. It's now a lively mix of museums, restaurants, and shops. The vibrant menu at Lake Avenue features fish caught right from Lake Superior. This hearty chowder is perfect with Chef Beran's Pepito Ancho Butter and Pumpkin Jam Sandwiches (see the recipe in the Main Courses section, page 106).

If you are not using the bones, skip this step and simply use 2 cups of vegetable stock (see below). If using the trout bones, rinse and dry them well. Place the bones on a baking sheet and roast at 350 degrees for 25 minutes. Place the roasted bones in a stockpot with the stock and bay leaves and bring to a boil. Immediately drop the heat and simmer for 30 minutes, occasionally skimming the surface with a ladle. Strain out the bones and bay leaves and reserve the liquid.

In a medium saucepan, melt 2 tablespoons of the butter over medium-low heat. Add the vegetables and herbs and sweat until the onions are translucent, about 10 minutes. Add the cream and turn up the heat to medium, simmering to reduce the volume of liquid by one-third.

In a sauté pan, melt 1 tablespoon of the butter over medium-high heat. Once the butter bubbles, add the trout fillet flesh side down and let it sear undisturbed until the edges are golden brown, about 4 minutes. Flip the trout and reduce the heat to medium. Add 2 cups of the trout bone stock (or vegetable stock) and simmer until reduced by half.

Carefully flake the fish with a fork and add the fish and liquid to the vegetable and cream mixture. Stir in the remaining 2 tablespoons of butter and season to taste with salt and pepper. Garnish with the reserved fennel fronds and serve with your favorite hot sauce and pepito and pumpkin jam sandwiches.

(see photograph on page 63)

4 whole heads garlic

¼ cup olive oil, divided

2 bunches stinging nettles,
    tough stems removed

1 leek, coarsely chopped

½ sweet onion, coarsely chopped

½ cup dry white wine

1 pint heavy cream

2 cups water

1 potato, peeled, small dice

¼ to ½ lemon, juiced

Salt and pepper to taste

Serves 4

Roasted Garlic and Nettle Soup

NOSH RESTAURANT AND BAR, LAKE CITY
CHEF AND OWNER GREG JAWORSKI

Walk along pretty much any fence line in early spring and you'll be sure to find some stinging nettles. (Take care to avoid sprayed areas.) You'll want to wear gloves when foraging for these beauties, but when cooked, these nutritious greens lose their sting. Nettles bring an almost teal-green color to this dish. The soup's subtle flavor is enhanced when prepared the day before serving.

Preheat the oven to 350 degrees.

Cut ½ inch off the top of each head of garlic, exposing the tops of the cloves. Lightly drizzle the garlic heads with 1 teaspoon of the olive oil and wrap snugly in aluminum foil, sealing well. Roast in the oven until the bulbs give freely when squeezed, 45 minutes to an hour. Remove from the oven and let cool.

Bring a small pot of water to a boil and prepare an ice bath. Wearing kitchen gloves to handle the nettles, drop them into the boiling water. Blanch for 10 seconds and then move to the ice bath to chill. This preserves the beautiful green color and neutralizes the plant's sting. Remove the leaves from the ice bath and squeeze the water from the leaves with your hands.

In a 2-quart saucepan, add the remaining olive oil to the pan over medium heat. Stir in the leek and onion and sweat gently until translucent; don't let them brown. Squeeze the roasted garlic from the heads and add to the pan. Add the white wine, reducing by half while stirring constantly. Next add the cream, water, and potato. Squeeze in the lemon juice, season with salt and pepper, and simmer until the potatoes are soft. Stir in the nettles and remove from heat.

In a blender, puree the soup in small batches until smooth. Serve warm.

❧ **Note:** *Chef Jaworski likes to swirl in a spoonful of kalamata olive tapenade. He says it "sounds weird, but the flavors rock together."*

1 large or 2 small kabocha
  or butternut squash

1 small sweet potato

2 tablespoons olive oil

¾ cup diced onion

¾ cup diced celery

2 small carrots, peeled and diced

5 cloves garlic

¼ cup brandy

2 quarts vegetable stock

1 cup whole milk

2 tablespoons saba

2 tablespoons hazelnut oil

Salt and pepper to taste

Garnish

2 tablespoons pumpkin seed oil

3 tablespoons toasted
  pumpkin seeds

2 tablespoons chopped fresh chives

Serves 6

Roasted Squash and Sweet Potato Soup with Hazelnut Oil and Saba

LUCIA'S RESTAURANT, MINNEAPOLIS ❧ CHEF RYAN LUND

Golden and creamy squash soup is an essential dish to have in your fall repertoire. The saba (a syrup made from grape juice or "must") adds a sweet raisin-y flavor, subtle and perfect with the squash.

Preheat the oven to 350 degrees.

Cut the squash in half and remove the seeds. With a fork, poke holes in the sweet potato. Place the squash and the sweet potato on a baking sheet and roast until tender, about 30 minutes.

Meanwhile, add the olive oil to a large stockpot and sauté the onion, celery, carrots, and garlic over medium–high heat. Deglaze the pan with the brandy and cook to reduce until dry.

When the squash is softened, allow to cool and scoop the flesh into the stockpot. Peel the sweet potato and add it in chunks to the pot. Pour in the vegetable stock and milk and simmer until all the vegetables are soft. Drizzle in the saba and hazelnut oil and season with salt and pepper.

In a blender, puree the soup in batches until smooth.

Serve warm in bowls garnished with a drizzle of pumpkin seed oil, toasted pumpkin seeds, and chopped chives.

¼ cup wild rice

1 pound kabocha (or other winter) squash

2 tablespoons extra virgin olive oil

1 small yellow onion, chopped

3 cloves garlic, minced

½ teaspoon chipotle pepper powder

1 teaspoon chili powder

1 teaspoon ground cumin

1 cup dry white wine

1 tablespoon fresh oregano, minced

1½ cups chopped fresh tomatoes, or 1 (15-ounce) can diced tomatoes with juice

1½ cups cooked kidney beans, or 1 (15-ounce) can kidney beans, drained

2 tablespoons tomato paste

1 teaspoon salt

Serves 4 to 6

Squash and Wild Rice Chili

COOKBOOK AUTHOR, TEACHER, AND PRIVATE CHEF, MINNEAPOLIS
CHEF ROBIN ASBELL

A longtime advocate for healthy eating, Chef Asbell has authored a variety of cookbooks including Big Vegan and Juice It. This hearty chili has a stick-to-your-ribs quality without any meat. Make a double batch and freeze it later to warm up on a chilly day.

Cook the wild rice in 1 cup water until tender, 20 to 40 minutes. Drain any excess water.

While the rice cooks, peel the squash, remove the seeds, and cut into 1-inch cubes. You should have about 2 cups. In a large pot, heat the olive oil over medium heat and sauté the onions until golden and tender. When the onions start to caramelize, add the garlic and sauté until fragrant. Add the spices and stir for 1 minute.

Add the squash cubes and stir to coat with the oil and spices. When they begin to stick to the pan, add the wine and oregano and stir to deglaze. Bring to a simmer, cover, and cook until the squash is tender when pierced with a knife, about 5 minutes.

Add the tomatoes, kidney beans, tomato paste, and salt. If the mixture is dry, add water or more wine. Stir in the cooked wild rice and simmer to heat through and meld flavors. Serve immediately.

Tomato-fennel soup

1 large onion, thinly sliced

1 tablespoon sugar

7 tablespoons olive oil

4 cloves garlic, thinly sliced

2 fennel bulbs, thinly sliced, green tops chopped and reserved for garnish

1 tablespoon fennel seed

2 tablespoons tomato paste

¼ cup Pernod

20 ounces tomato puree

2 cups vegetable stock

2 tablespoons butter

Salt and pepper to taste

"Inside out" grilled cheese sandwiches

2 tablespoons butter, softened

4 slices white pullman loaf bread

2 slices Gruyère cheese, cut in half

2 slices Fontina cheese, cut in half

2 slices pepper Jack cheese, cut in half

¼ cup goat cheese crumbles

½ cup grated Cheddar cheese

Tomato-Fennel Soup with "Inside Out" Grilled Cheese Sandwiches

VICTORY 44, MINNEAPOLIS
CHEF AND OWNER ERICK HARCEY

What is more comforting than creamy tomato soup and a grilled cheese sandwich? Try this combo that takes classic tomato soup up a notch with the addition of fennel. The "inside out" sandwich sounds trickier than it is—crispy cheesy outside and creamy cheesy inside.

For the tomato-fennel soup:
Toss the onion slices with the sugar in a small bowl. Heat the olive oil in a large saucepan and sauté the onion, garlic, fennel, and fennel seed until golden. Add the tomato paste and cook for a few minutes more while stirring continually. Deglaze with the Pernod. Stir in the tomato puree and vegetable stock and simmer until the vegetables are tender, about 25 minutes.

Puree in a blender until smooth. Blend in the 2 tablespoons of butter and season with salt and pepper to taste. Keep the soup warm while you prepare the sandwiches.

For the "inside out" grilled cheese sandwiches:
Preheat a large griddle or cast-iron pan on medium heat. Butter one side of each slice of bread and brown on the griddle. Top each with the Gruyère, Fontina, pepper Jack, and goat cheese. Once the cheese is slightly melted, remove the bread from the skillet and divide the grated Cheddar into four spots on the griddle. Top each of the Cheddar spots with the slices of bread. Let the cheeses melt as the Cheddar gets crispy. Fold each over to form a sandwich and slice in half.

Lemon-fennel whipped cream garnish

1 lemon, zested and juiced

Chopped fennel greens

½ cup heavy cream, whipped

Serves 4

For the lemon-fennel whipped cream garnish:
In a small bowl, stir the lemon juice and zest and reserved green tops of the fennel into the whipped cream. Refrigerate until ready to serve.

Garnish each bowl of soup with a dollop of the lemon–fennel whipped cream.

Wild Hare
Smoky Squash Chowder

WILD HARE BISTRO, BEMIDJI
CHEF AND OWNER MONI SCHNEIDER

This recipe was created out of necessity. The restaurant had piles of sweet, delicious butternut squash coming in from Clearwater Pigcraft farm, one of their local suppliers. Chef Schneider's inspired blend of spices gives this chowder a warmth that's perfect for chilly fall evenings.

1 ½ to 2 pounds butternut squash, cut in half, seeds removed

2 tablespoons butter or olive oil

1 yellow onion, small dice (about 1 cup)

2 ribs celery, small dice

4 cloves garlic, minced

1 teaspoon paprika

1 teaspoon smoked Spanish paprika

½ teaspoon ground coriander

½ teaspoon ground cumin

½ teaspoon ground turmeric

¼ teaspoon liquid smoke

4 cups vegetable or chicken broth

1 pound heirloom potatoes, peeled and chopped

½ cup heavy cream

3 ounces smoked Gouda cheese, shredded

Salt and pepper to taste

Preheat the oven to 350 degrees.

Place the squash halves on a lightly oiled baking sheet and roast until softened and the edges are caramelized, 45 to 60 minutes. Allow the squash to cool, scrape out the soft flesh, and reserve.

Heat the butter or olive oil in a large soup pot and sauté the onions along with a pinch of salt until they soften and begin to brown. Add the celery and continue to stir occasionally until softened and nicely browned. Add the garlic and spices, stirring occasionally until fragrant, 2 to 3 minutes. Add the liquid smoke, broth, potatoes, and another pinch of salt. Simmer, covered, until the potatoes are cooked through. Add the roasted squash, heavy cream, and shredded cheese.

Use a potato masher to combine all the ingredients, breaking up the potatoes and squash to achieve a chunky, but not too thick, consistency. Add additional water or broth if needed. Season to taste with salt and pepper and serve hot.

Serves 6 to 8

Cocktails

Dashfire Bitters "New Fashioned," p. 79

Beebopareebop Strawberry Rhubarb Cocktail

VIKRE DISTILLERY, DULUTH ❧   COFOUNDER EMILY VIKRE

Garrison Keillor sings a ditty about Beebopareebop rhubarb pie, crooning "one little thing can revive a guy." Well, this cocktail also has restorative properties, with gin that's distilled near the shores of the great Lake Superior and punctuated with local flavors, including wild berries, sumac, juniper, spruce tips, cedar wood, and even rhubarb. When you infuse this gin with fresh berries and shake it together with rhubarb syrup, you'll be singing the "Beebopareebop" tune too!

Strawberry-infused gin

2 cups Vikre Boreal Cedar Gin

1 cup hulled and quartered fresh strawberries

Rhubarb syrup

1 cup (8 ounces) chopped fresh rhubarb

1 cup sugar

1 cup boiling water

The cocktail

2 ounces strawberry-infused Vikre Boreal Cedar Gin

1 ounce rhubarb syrup

¾ ounce lemon juice

Fresh strawberry, for garnish

Makes 1 cocktail

For the strawberry-infused gin:
Combine the gin and strawberries in an airtight container and let stand for 48 hours. Strain through a fine-mesh strainer and store in an airtight container indefinitely. This makes 2 cups of infused gin.

For the rhubarb syrup:
Combine the rhubarb and sugar in a blender. Pour the boiling water over the mixture, cover, and blend until smooth, about 1 minute. Strain the rhubarb mixture through a fine-mesh strainer, pressing gently on the pulp to get all the liquid out. Discard the pulp, trans- fer the rhubarb syrup to an airtight container, and refrigerate. This makes about 2 cups of rhubarb syrup, which will keep for a couple of weeks refrigerated.

For the cocktail:
In a cocktail shaker with ice, combine 2 ounces of the strawberry- infused gin, 1 ounce rhubarb syrup, and the lemon juice and shake vigorously until well chilled. Strain into a cocktail glass and garnish with a fresh strawberry.

Oversize shard of ice, for serving

2 ounces 11 Wells Bourbon

¼ ounce simple syrup

3 to 5 drops Dashfire Vintage
  Orange Bitters

Pinch smoked sea salt

Orange twist, for garnish

Makes 1 cocktail

Dashfire Bitters "New Fashioned"

DASHFIRE BITTERS, ST. PAUL   ❧   OWNER LEE EGBERT

11 Wells Bourbon is the first Minnesota-made bourbon. Swirl, sniff, and sip this drink by a fire and appreciate the subtle flavors added by the aromatic bitters and a hint of smoke from the sea salt.

Place an oversize piece of clear ice in a lowball glass. (To make shards, buy or freeze a block of ice, then score and break it with an ice pick.) In a mixing glass, stir the bourbon, simple syrup, bitters, and sea salt to combine. Pour over the ice in the lowball glass. Garnish with an orange twist.

Cucumber water

½ cucumber, peeled and seeded

2 tablespoons water

The cosmopolitan

2 ounces Solveig Gin

1 ounce triple sec

½ ounce fresh lime juice

½ ounce cucumber water

½ ounce cranberry juice

Ice cubes

Orange twist, for garnish

Makes 1 cocktail

Får North Spirits
Cucumber Cosmopolitan

FÅR NORTH SPIRITS, HALLOCK
FOUNDING PARTNERS MICHAEL SWANSON AND CHERI REESE

*Cool as a cucumber, this cocktail refreshes on a hot summer evening.
Prepare the cucumber water in advance and keep it chilled and ready
for this midsummer drink.*

For the cucumber water:
In a blender, puree the cucumber with the water until smooth. Strain
through a fine-mesh strainer or cheesecloth. Reserve the liquid and
chill in the refrigerator until ready to use. Use within 2 to 3 days.

For the cosmopolitan:
In a cocktail shaker with ice, combine the gin, triple sec, lime juice,
½ ounce of cucumber water, and cranberry juice and shake until well
chilled. Strain and pour into a coup or martini glass and garnish with
an orange twist.

Ice cubes

1 ½ ounces Ålander Spiced Rum

1 ounce cachaça

1 ounce pineapple juice

½ ounce triple sec

Splash of Rose's Lime juice

Splash of Rose's Grenadine

Splash of ginger ale

Orange slice, for garnish

Cinnamon stick, for garnish

Makes 1 cocktail

Får North Spirits
Oak Island Rum Punch

FÅR NORTH SPIRITS, HALLOCK
FOUNDING PARTNERS MICHAEL SWANSON AND CHERI REESE

This is Får North's signature rum drink. The calligraphic pattern on the bottle is actually a topographical map of Oak Island at Lake of the Woods in northern Minnesota. It's a perfect summer sipper for enjoying "island life"!

Put the ice cubes in a tall glass. Add the rum, cachaça, pineapple juice, triple sec, lime juice, grenadine, and ginger ale and stir. Garnish with an orange slice and a cinnamon stick.

1 ½ ounces Norseman
    Strawberry Rhubarb Gin

1 ounce lemon juice

1 ounce simple syrup

Dry sparkling wine, such as cava
    or champagne, to fill glass

Lemon twist, for garnish

Strawberry slice, for garnish

Makes 1 cocktail

Norseman Strawberry Rhubarb Fizz

A PROPER POUR, MINNEAPOLIS   &   OWNER JASON SUSS

A truly Minnesotan gin delicately flavored with strawberries and rhubarb serves up an homage to springtime. Because of its seasonal nature, this gin is in limited supply, so grab it when you are able. This is a subtly flavored drink, just like the subtle colors and smells of spring.

In a cocktail shaker with ice, combine the gin, lemon juice, and simple syrup. Shake until well chilled, about 5 seconds. Add an ounce or two of the sparkling wine. Strain into a champagne flute and then top with more sparkling wine. (Adding the sparkling wine to the shaker first ensures the drink is well mixed and also prevents foaming when you top it with more sparkling wine.) Garnish with a lemon twist and a strawberry slice.

2 ounces Vikre Boreal Cedar Gin

¾ ounce grade B maple syrup

¾ ounce lemon juice

3 dashes aromatic bitters,
    like Dashfire Brandy Old
    Fashioned or Bittercube Trinity

3 ounces very dry hard cider,
    like 12 Ciderhouse

Makes 1 cocktail

Nothing Gold Can Stay

VIKRE DISTILLERY, DULUTH   ❧   COFOUNDER EMILY VIKRE

This drink is inspired by a poem by Robert Frost titled "Nothing Gold Can Stay," reflecting on the change of seasons. Crisp, dry cider and smoky sweet maple syrup make this a perfectly poetic cocktail for early autumn sipping.

In a cocktail shaker with ice, combine the gin, maple syrup, lemon juice, and bitters. Shake until well chilled, then strain into a glass and top with the hard cider.

1 ½ ounces Fitzgerald Gin

1 ounce cranberry juice

¼ ounce lime juice

¼ ounce simple syrup

Pinch sea salt

Lime slice, for garnish

Makes 1 cocktail

Steady Eddie

DU NORD CRAFT SPIRITS, MINNEAPOLIS
HEAD DISTILLER AND OWNER CHRIS MONTANA

At Du Nord, they use grains that are grown in Minnesota. After distilling, the grains go to feed livestock. Visit their tasting room and schedule a distillery tour to see the process and sample their products.

In a cocktail shaker with ice, combine the gin, cranberry juice, lime juice, simple syrup, and salt. Shake and strain into a lowball glass over ice. Garnish with a slice of lime.

Main
Courses

Bison Burger, p. 87

Beef Wellington with Swiss Chard and Mushroom Duxelles

FOREPAUGH'S, ST. PAUL ❧ CHEF DONALD GONZALES

Old-school favorites like beef Wellington are standards at Forepaugh's in historic St. Paul. Chef Gonzales, having trained with some of the nation's finest chefs, forges his own culinary concepts, creating classic American cuisine with global influences.

Mushroom duxelles

1 tablespoon butter

5 cups sliced button mushrooms

3 tablespoons fresh lemon juice

1 ½ teaspoons fresh thyme leaves

1 teaspoon finely chopped
     fresh parsley

½ Thai chile pepper, minced

1 tablespoon kosher salt

Pepper to taste

Beef Wellington

1 bunch Swiss chard

4 (5-ounce each) beef tenderloins,
     cut for filet mignon

Salt and pepper

2 tablespoons high-heat cooking oil

1 sheet (½ pound) puff pastry

1 egg

Serves 4

For the mushroom duxelles:
Melt the butter in a large skillet over medium heat and sauté the mushrooms until golden brown, 15 to 20 minutes. Deglaze with the lemon juice and add the thyme, parsley, red chile, salt, and pepper. Place the mixture in the bowl of a food processor and process until it is the consistency of coarse cornmeal. Refrigerate until ready to use.

For the beef Wellington:
Preheat the oven to 425 degrees.

Remove the tough stems from the Swiss chard. Fill a bowl with water and ice cubes. In a medium pot, bring 1 quart of water to a boil and submerge the chard. When the water returns to a boil, time the chard for 2 minutes, then remove and submerge in the ice water bath. When well chilled, remove and dry on a towel.

Season the beef portions with salt and pepper to taste and sear in a hot pan drizzled with high-heat cooking oil. Sear both sides of the filets and set aside to cool. When cooled to room temperature, top each filet with the mushroom duxelle and wrap the filets with the blanched Swiss chard leaves. Wrap with plastic wrap and refrigerate.

Cut the puff pastry into four even portions. On a lightly floured board, roll out the four pieces so they are big enough to wrap entirely around the filets. Cut 1-inch slits in the pastry sheets so the Swiss chard will show through the pastry. Wrap each filet with a piece of pastry and transfer to a parchment-lined baking sheet. Beat the egg and brush it onto each of the pastry blankets. Bake in the oven until the pastry is golden brown, 15 to 20 minutes. Serve immediately.

1 ¾ pounds ground bison chuck, chilled

½ cup (1 stick) butter, chilled and minced

5 tablespoons minced shallot

3 medium cloves garlic, minced

6 brioche buns

¼ cup (½ stick) butter, softened

Sea salt to taste

Serves 6

Bison Burger

HELL'S KITCHEN, MINNEAPOLIS   ❧   CHEF MITCH OMER

"Bison is one of the greatest red meats around, and a valid reason for abandoning vegetarianism," says Chef Omer. Bison is leaner than either beef or chicken; Chef Omer compensates for this by folding unsalted butter into the ground bison chuck. It's no wonder this burger outsells all other burgers on the Hell's Kitchen menu.

Mix the bison and butter together in a chilled bowl, then gently mix in the shallot and garlic. Mix until evenly blended, but be careful not to compact the meat. Gently form six patties.

Grill, or cook the patties in a cast-iron skillet or griddle over medium-high heat. (For grilling, place the meat about 4 inches from the heat and use low flame or hot coals.) Cooking times will vary depending on the thickness of your patties. Once the burgers are on the grill or griddle, don't press down on them. Turn each burger only once, and cook evenly on both sides, reducing the heat after the second side has seared. Cook to desired doneness (an internal temperature of 160 degrees is considered safest).

Split the buns, slather the faces with the softened butter, and place face down on the grill or griddle. Toast until golden brown.

Taste the burger before you season it with salt to taste.

❧ **Note:** *Garnish your burger à la Hell's Kitchen with bacon, sautéed mushrooms and onions, jalapeños, or guacamole, and your choice of melted cheese.*

(see photograph on page 85)

Braised Beef Pot Roast

CAFE LEVAIN, MINNEAPOLIS ❧ CHEF ADAM VICKERMAN

It has been said, "Well-fed people never mind the weather." Pot roast is a dish that makes one welcome winter; the warm smells of pot roast braising in the oven are perfect for chilly days. Low and slow is the way to go with this comforting classic. Chef Vickerman favors grass-fed roasts from Thousand Hills Cattle Company in Cannon Falls. This roast pairs well with Roasted Root Vegetables (see the recipe in Salads and Sides section, page 58).

1 (24-ounce) beef pot roast

Salt and pepper to taste

1 tablespoon canola oil

2 carrots, peeled, rough dice

4 stalks celery, rough dice

2 yellow onions, peeled, rough dice

1 bottle port wine

1 bottle red wine

1 head garlic, halved

¼ cup black peppercorns

2 fresh bay leaves

1 bunch fresh thyme

2 sprigs fresh rosemary

1 (20-ounce) can crushed
     San Marzano tomatoes

¼ cup balsamic vinegar

1 teaspoon to 2 tablespoons
     red chili flakes, to taste

4 cups (1 quart) beef stock

Serves 4 to 6

Preheat the oven to 300 degrees.

Pat the meat dry with paper towels and season with salt and pepper. Heat the canola oil in a Dutch oven over high heat and sear the pot roast on all sides until well caramelized. Remove the meat and add the carrots, celery, and onion and sauté until softened. Remove the vegetables and deglaze the pan with half of the port wine, then reduce to a simmer. Add the remaining port and red wine and simmer until reduced by half.

Add the meat and vegetables back to the Dutch oven along with the garlic, peppercorns, herbs, tomatoes, vinegar, and chili flakes. Pour the beef stock over all to cover, and place the pan in the oven for 3 to 5 hours. Check the meat after 3 hours and turn over in the pan. When the meat is tender, remove it from the braising liquid. Strain the liquid, pressing the flavor from the vegetables and herbs. If you are making this the day ahead of serving, place the meat in the strained liquid and refrigerate overnight, which will make it easier to skim off the fat.

When ready to eat, place the roast in half of the braising liquid and heat gently to warm the roast. Reduce the other half of the liquid until it is a nice syrupy glaze. Serve the roast sliced and glazed with the reduced sauce.

Braised duck legs

2 medium carrots, peeled,

1 large onion, peeled

1 stalk celery

4 fresh duck legs, skin on, trimmed

Salt and pepper

2 sprigs fresh sage

2 sprigs fresh thyme

2 (2-inch-long) orange peels, pith removed

6 black peppercorns, cracked

⅓ cup port

½ cup red wine

4 cups (1 quart) chicken stock, divided

2 tablespoons butter

Creamy farro

1 cup farro

½ cup heavy cream

½ cup orange juice

2 tablespoons mascarpone cheese

3 tablespoons grated Parmesan cheese, divided

1 tablespoon fresh orange zest

Braised Duck Legs with Creamy Farro and Orange

SPOON AND STABLE RESTAURANT, MINNEAPOLIS
CHEF GAVIN KAYSEN

A Minnesota native, Chef Kaysen has returned to his midwestern roots after a prestigious career at Café Boulud in New York City. This dish features farro, an ancient strain of wheat, which gives a nod to the important role of wheat production in Minnesota history.

For the braised duck legs:
Preheat the oven to 325 degrees.

Cut one carrot, half the onion, and the celery into a medium dice. Julienne the remaining carrot and onion half.

Generously season the duck legs on all sides with salt and pepper. Heat a 3-quart, oven-safe sauté pan over medium-high heat and add the duck legs skin-side down in one layer. Sear until golden brown, about 3 minutes, then flip and brown the other side for another 3 minutes. Remove the legs from the pan, reduce the heat to medium-low, and discard all but about 2 tablespoons of the fat from the pan.

Add the medium-dice vegetables, sage, thyme, orange peels, and peppercorns to the pan. Sprinkle with salt and pepper. Cook, stirring, until the onions are translucent, about 4 minutes. Add the port and wine and simmer until reduced by half. Return the duck legs to the pan with 3 cups of the chicken stock. Bring to a simmer, cover, and transfer to the oven. Braise, covered, for 2 hours. Transfer the duck legs to a plate to cool. When the duck legs are cool enough to handle, pick off the meat and discard the skin and bones.

(continued on page 90)

Orange garnish

2 oranges

2 bunches watercress

Salt and freshly ground
    white pepper to taste

Serves 4

Strain the braising liquid remaining in the pan through a fine-meshed sieve and skim off as much fat as possible, reserving the liquid. Wipe the pan clean, return it to medium-low heat, and add the butter. Add the julienned vegetables with a sprinkling of salt and pepper and cook, stirring, until soft. Remove the vegetables and set aside.

For the creamy farro:
Add the reserved braising liquid to the same pan, along with the farro and cream. Simmer for 35 to 45 minutes, stirring occasionally and adding the remaining cup of chicken stock in intervals if needed. Cook until the farro is tender, moist, and soft to the bite.

Add the duck meat, reserved onion and carrot, orange juice, mascarpone cheese, 2 tablespoons of the Parmesan cheese, and orange zest to the farro. Combine well and check seasoning.

For the orange garnish:
Peel the oranges and break into segments. Rinse and destem the watercress.

To assemble:
Serve the braised duck and farro in shallow bowls, topped with orange segments, watercress leaves, the remaining Parmesan cheese, and salt and white pepper to taste.

Braised pork shank ossobuco

6 to 8 pork shanks, 2½- to 3-inch "ossobuco" crosscut pieces

Salt and pepper to taste

¼ cup olive oil

3 small red onions

3 carrots, peeled

3 stalks celery

3 cloves garlic, minced

Pinch crushed red pepper flakes

3 anchovy fillets

4 sprigs fresh rosemary

8 sprigs fresh thyme

2 cups dry white wine

3 cups chicken stock

1 (28-ounce) can whole plum tomatoes

Herb gremolata

¼ cup fresh parsley leaves

2 lemons, zested

2 cloves garlic

½ teaspoon crushed red pepper flakes

2 tablespoons fresh rosemary leaves

2 tablespoons fresh thyme leaves

Serves 4 to 6

Braised Pork Shank Ossobuco with Herb Gremolata (Ossobuco di Maiale)

TERZO, MINNEAPOLIS   CHEF THOMAS BRODER

Terzo makes a modern version of the Italian classic veal ossobuco that instead highlights Minnesota's bounty of fresh pork. Have a butcher crosscut Duroc pork shanks into 2½- to 3-inch pieces, revealing the bone marrow. Slow braising with aromatic vegetables, herbs, and wine yields a rich and tender dish. Serve with soft polenta and a drizzle of extra virgin olive oil.

For the braised pork shank ossobuco:
Preheat the oven to 350 degrees.

Dry the pork shanks and tie each piece with butcher's twine. Season the meat generously with salt and pepper. Heat the olive oil in a braising pan large enough to cook the pork shanks and not be over-crowded. Sear the pork pieces until golden brown on all sides, then remove from the pan and set aside.

Pour off the excess fat from the pan. Slice the onions, carrots, and celery into ¼-inch dice. Over medium heat, sweat diced vegetables for 5 minutes. Add the minced garlic, red pepper flakes, and anchovy fillets and cook for 3 more minutes. Stir in the rosemary and thyme sprigs, then deglaze with the wine, scraping the browned bits from the pan and reducing until the pan is almost dry. Add the chicken stock and tomatoes and return the pork to the pan.

Bring to a simmer, cover tightly with foil, and place in the oven for 4 hours. Remove the pan from the oven. The pork should be very tender. If you are making this the day before serving, cool for 1 hour and refrigerate overnight. The following day you can remove the congealed fat and the pork from the pan and run the braising liquid and vegetables through a food mill to make the sauce. If you are making the sauce on the day of braising, do your best to skim off the fat. Bring the sauce to a simmer and adjust seasonings to taste. Add the pork pieces to the sauce to reheat the pork.

For the herb gremolata:
On a cutting board, chop the parsley, lemon zest, garlic, and herbs together.

To assemble:
Cut the twine from the pork shanks and spoon the sauce over the meat. Serve with soft polenta and sprinkle with the herb gremolata.

Turkey

1 large (14-pound) turkey

Brine

1 gallon water

1 cup kosher salt

1 head garlic, halved crosswise

4 fresh bay leaves

1 yellow onion, halved

1 tablespoon black peppercorns

1 tablespoon yellow mustard seed

1 tablespoon fennel seed

1 gallon ice water

Caramelized salsify

4 quarts water

1 lemon, juiced

2 pounds salsify

½ teaspoon salt

¼ teaspoon pepper

2 cups dry white wine

5 sprigs fresh thyme

2 bay leaves

4 cloves garlic, lightly crushed

½ cup (1 stick) butter

Brined Turkey with Pan Jus and Caramelized Salsify

SALT CELLAR, ST. PAUL   &   CHEF ALAN BERGO

For a perfectly moist and flavorful bird, brine the turkey the night before roasting. Look for salsify at farmers' markets and specialty grocers.

For the turkey:
Allow the turkey to thaw completely in the refrigerator. Remove the innards and reserve the neck and gizzard for the jus.

For the brine:
Bring the gallon of water to a boil and stir in the salt, garlic, bay leaves, onion, peppercorns, and mustard and fennel seed. Stir until the salt is dissolved, then remove from heat and add the gallon of ice water. When the brine is cool, add the turkey, cover, and refrigerate for 24 hours. If needed, weight the turkey to keep it submerged in the brine.

To roast the turkey:
Preheat the oven to 450 degrees. Remove the turkey from the brine, allow to drain, and place in a large roasting pan with a rack. Roast until the skin is golden, about 45 minutes. Reduce the heat to 300 degrees and continue roasting the turkey until the juices in the legs run clear when pierced with a knife, another 2 to 3 hours. Remove the turkey from the oven and allow to rest while you prepare the pan jus.

For the caramelized salsify:
Prepare acidulated water by putting 1 quart of water in a bowl and adding the lemon juice. Peel the salsify and add it to the water as you go so it doesn't discolor. When all the salsify is peeled, transfer it to a small stockpot with 3 quarts water, salt, pepper, white wine, herbs, and garlic. Bring the water to a boil, then reduce the heat to a simmer and cook until the salsify is very tender, about 45 minutes.

Pan jus

1 tablespoon butter

1 tablespoon flour

1 cup dry white wine

6 cups chicken stock,
preferably homemade

½ cup heavy cream

1 tablespoon chopped fresh
thyme leaves

Kosher salt and ground
white pepper to taste

Serves 10 to 12, with leftovers

Remove the salsify from the pot and dry thoroughly on paper towels. In a large pan or skillet on medium heat, melt the butter, add the salsify, and cook, stirring occasionally, until golden brown and caramelized. Remove the salsify to a serving dish, discarding excess fat.

For the pan jus:
Knead the butter and flour together to make a smooth paste; set aside. Place the roasting pan from the turkey on a stove burner and deglaze the pan with the wine, scraping up the brown bits. When the wine is almost completely evaporated, add the chicken stock and cook until reduced by half. Whisk in the kneaded butter and flour and continue cooking until thickened. Add the cream and season with the thyme, salt, and pepper; keep warm.

Carve the turkey onto a platter and serve with the pan jus and caramelized salsify.

Pickled ramps

1 pound ramp bulbs

3 cups water

1 tablespoon kosher salt

½ cup sugar

1½ cups apple cider vinegar

Aioli

¼ cup pickled ramps

¼ cup ramp pickling juice

½ cup mayonnaise

Cornmeal sunfish

¾ cup finely ground cornmeal

¼ cup coarsely ground cornmeal

½ teaspoon paprika

½ teaspoon dried thyme

Cayenne pepper to taste

Salt and pepper to taste

¼ cup grape seed oil

6 ounces sunfish fillets (6 to 8 fillets)

2 tablespoons butter

Serves 2

Cornmeal Sunfish
with Pickled Ramp Aioli

SALT CELLAR, ST. PAUL   ❧   CHEF ALAN BERGO

Could there be anything better than catching panfish right off the dock and then taking them into the kitchen to cook? Chef Bergo, known as "The Forager Chef," specializes in just such fresh-from-nature dishes. In early spring, his favorite forest find is ramps, also called wild leeks. Pickling them preserves their flavor long after their short season has passed.

For the pickled ramps:
Trim the taproots off the ramp bulbs, but leave the red portion of the stem attached.

Put the water, salt, and sugar in a large pot over medium heat. When the mixture starts to steam, add the ramps and cover, making sure the lid is on tight. Reduce the heat to low and steam the ramp bulbs until they are wilted but still a bit crunchy in the middle, about 5 minutes. After the ramps are par cooked, add the vinegar. Pack pint jars full of this mixture and process them in a water bath canner for 15 minutes. Alternatively, store the ramps covered in their liquid in the refrigerator.

For the aioli:
Combine the pickled ramps with the pickling juice. Simmer together until the pan is nearly dry. Cool, stir in the mayonnaise, and set aside.

For the cornmeal sunfish:
In a large bowl, combine the fine and coarse cornmeals and stir in the paprika, thyme, cayenne pepper, salt, and pepper. Heat the oil in a large cast-iron skillet. Dredge the sunfish fillets in the cornmeal. When the oil is nearly smoking, add the sunfish, skin side down, and cook until golden brown. Add the butter and reduce the heat to medium, then flip the sunfish over to lightly cook on the other side. Be careful not to overcook the fish. Serve with the pickled ramp aioli.

Rhubarb barbecue sauce

3 cups chopped rhubarb

⅓ cup minced yellow onion

2 tablespoons minced fresh ginger root

1 jalapeño pepper, minced

½ cup real maple syrup

½ cup apple cider vinegar

¼ cup molasses

2 tablespoons mustard powder

1 tablespoon ground coriander

1 tablespoon smoked Spanish paprika

1 teaspoon kosher salt

¼ teaspoon pepper

Grilled chicken

1 fryer (3 to 4 pounds) chicken

Salt and pepper to taste

Serves 4 to 6

Grilled Chicken with Rhubarb Barbecue Sauce

THAT FOOD GIRL, MINNEAPOLIS ❧ CHEF BETSY NELSON

Rhubarb is one of the first harvestable crops that pop up in my garden, and after a long winter we are hungry for the flavor of something home-grown. When rhubarb is abundant, make this savory sauce to slather on grilled chicken, beef, pork, or fish.

For the rhubarb barbecue sauce:
In a medium, heavy saucepan over medium-low heat, combine the rhubarb, onion, ginger, and jalapeño (remove the seeds if you want a less spicy sauce). Stir in the maple syrup, vinegar, and molasses. Add the spices, salt, and pepper and simmer, stirring occasionally to prevent sticking, until thickened, 30 to 45 minutes. Taste to check flavor and adjust as needed with salt and pepper. Cool and refrigerate until ready to use. This sauce keeps well for 3 to 4 weeks.

For the grilled chicken:
Preheat the grill. Cut the chicken into pieces and season with the salt and pepper. Arrange the chicken on the hot grill and cook for 15 to 20 minutes, turning occasionally and adjusting the heat to cook the chicken evenly. In the last 5 minutes of grilling, brush the chicken with the rhubarb barbecue sauce. Remove from the grill when the chicken reaches an internal temperature of 165 degrees. Serve with extra barbecue sauce for dipping.

Sweet corn relish

4 ears sweet corn, shucked

2 teaspoons fine sea salt

2 tablespoons apple cider vinegar

2 tablespoons grape seed oil

1 tablespoon walnut oil

¼ cup diced (⅛ inch) sweet onions

¼ cup bias sliced (⅛ inch)
   green onions

1 teaspoon minced fresh garlic

2 tablespoons chopped fresh
   rosemary

½ teaspoon pepper

Grilled Minnesota pork loin

2-pound boneless naturally
   raised pork loin, trimmed

1 ounce fresh rosemary, chopped

1 ounce fresh lavender, chopped

2 tablespoons grape seed oil

2 teaspoons fine sea salt

½ teaspoon pepper

Serves 4 to 6

Grilled Minnesota Pork Loin with Sweet Corn Relish

HEARTLAND RESTAURANT, ST. PAUL   ❧   CHEF LENNY RUSSO

Chef Russo created this recipe for a demo at the Minnesota State Fair during sweet corn's peak season. The sweet-crisp corn relish brightens the smoky, savory pork loin.

For the sweet corn relish:
Cut the corn kernels off the cobs and cook them in salted boiling water for 7 minutes. While the corn is cooking, dissolve the salt in the vinegar in a mixing bowl. Whisk in the oils. Drain the corn from the boiling water and add to the mixing bowl. Add the onions, garlic, rosemary, and pepper. Blend well and set aside.

For the grilled Minnesota pork loin:
Season the pork with the rosemary, lavender, oil, salt, and pepper. Grill the pork over moderate heat for 4 minutes on each side. Allow to rest for 10 minutes and then slice into portions.

Divide the corn relish onto plates and top with the pork. Serve immediately.

1 bunch asparagus

8 spring onions

4 lamb chops

Salt and pepper to taste

2 tablespoons sunflower oil

Pinch each chopped fresh chives,
    thyme, and parsley

1 cup white wine

½ cup (1 stick) butter

Balsamic reduction
    (optional; see Note)

Serves 4

Lamb Chops with Spring Vegetables

THE CURIOUS GOAT, MINNEAPOLIS   ❧   CHEF IAN GRAY

You can often find The Curious Goat truck parked outside Sociable Cider Werks, whose cider and beer are inspired pairings for their food. Lamb chops, the classiest "fast food," can go from kitchen to table in about fifteen minutes. Chef Gray likes to get his lamb from Braucher's Sunshine Harvest Farm near Webster and sunflower oil from Smude's near Pierz.

Preheat the oven to 400 degrees.

Trim the woody ends off the asparagus. Coarsely chop the onions.

Season the lamb chops with salt and pepper. Heat an oven-safe sauté pan, add the oil, and sauté the lamb chops over medium-high heat on one side for 4 minutes. Turn the chops over and add the asparagus and onions. Put the pan in the oven for 6 to 7 minutes. Remove the pan from the oven, then remove the chops from the pan and allow to rest.

Place the pan back on the stovetop at medium heat and add the chives, thyme, and parsley. Deglaze with the wine and swirl in the butter. Season with salt and pepper to taste.

Place a lamb chop on each plate and serve with the asparagus, onions, and sauce. Drizzle with balsamic reduction if desired.

❧ **Note:** *Making a balsamic reduction is simple enough, but you'll want to turn the range fan on high to vent the potent vinegar fumes. In a medium stainless steel pan, bring 1 cup of balsamic vinegar to a simmer over medium-high heat. Lower the heat to hold at a low simmer and cook until reduced by half. Remove from heat and let cool.*

Lamb meatballs

1 pound ground lamb

½ pound ground pork

1 egg

2 tablespoons whole milk

½ tablespoon garlic powder

1 teaspoon crushed red
    pepper flakes

½ teaspoon ground cinnamon

1 teaspoon herbs de Provence

½ teaspoon ground ginger

1 teaspoon paprika

Salt and pepper to taste

Soft polenta

1 cup whole milk

1 cup heavy cream

1 cup water

1 cup stone-ground polenta

2 ounces shredded Parmesan cheese

½ lemon, juiced

Salt and pepper to taste

Red pepper jus

4 red bell peppers

½ ounce sherry vinegar

1 tablespoon sugar

Salt to taste

Lamb Meatballs with Soft Polenta, Red Pepper Jus, and Parsley-Red Onion Salad

ZZEST CAFÉ, ROCHESTER   ❧   CHEF JUSTIN SCHOVILLE

Zzest started as a small market and café that has grown quickly into a full-blown restaurant and bar. The creamy polenta in this dish makes a great stage for the "zzesty" meatballs and tangy salad and sauce. Prepare the meatballs a day or two ahead for better flavor.

For the lamb meatballs:
Preheat the oven to 400 degrees. In a large bowl, mix together the ground lamb and pork, then work in the egg, milk, herbs, and spices until well combined. Shape the mixture with your hands into thirty-six meatballs. Arrange on a baking sheet and bake until cooked through, 14 to 16 minutes.

For the soft polenta:
Add the milk, heavy cream, and water to a large pot and bring to a simmer over medium heat. Whisk in the polenta and return to a simmer. Cook for 10 minutes, stirring frequently. Remove from heat, cover with a lid, and let thicken until soft, about 15 minutes. Stir in the Parmesan cheese and lemon juice and season with salt and pepper.

For the red pepper jus:
Run the whole red peppers through a juicer and pour into a small pot over medium heat. Add the sherry vinegar, sugar, and salt and simmer until syrupy, 8 to 10 minutes. Remove from heat.

(continued on page 102)

Parsley-red onion salad

1 bunch Italian parsley,
   leaves picked off
   with some stems

½ red onion, sliced thin

1 tablespoon sherry vinegar

1 tablespoon extra virgin olive oil

Salt and pepper to taste

Serves 6

For the parsley-red onion salad:
In a medium bowl, toss the parsley and onion together with the vinegar and olive oil. Season with salt and pepper to taste.

To assemble:
Divide the polenta into six bowls. Top each with five or six meatballs and drizzle with the red pepper jus. Garnish with the parsley–red onion salad.

Olivada

1 cup pitted Ligurian black olives

2 teaspoons chopped garlic

1 tablespoon chopped fresh parsley

1 tablespoon chopped fresh basil

2 teaspoons brine-packed capers,
   rinsed and drained

¼ cup extra virgin olive oil

Linguine

1 pound linguine

2 tablespoons butter

4 tablespoons olivada

1 cup heavy cream

4 tablespoons grated Parmigiano-
   Reggiano cheese

3 tablespoons chopped fresh
   Italian parsley

Serves 4 to 6

Linguine Bianco e Nero

BRODERS' RESTAURANT, MINNEAPOLIS
CHEF THOMAS BRODER

*The elegance of this dish lies in the simple integrity of the "black and white"
ingredients. You can find the Ligurian olives, linguine, and Parmigiano at
Broders' Cucina Italiana, an Italian market and deli.*

For the olivada:
Combine the olives, garlic, parsley, basil, and capers in a food processor. Drizzle in the olive oil and process to form a smooth paste. Add
a little more oil if needed.

For the linguine:
Bring a large pot of water to a boil. Add the linguine noodles to the
boiling water and return to a boil. Cook until the pasta is al dente,
8 to 10 minutes.

While the linguine is cooking, in a large braising pan, melt the butter
over low heat. Add 4 tablespoons of the olivada and whisk to combine. Stir in the cream and simmer slowly to slightly thicken. Add
the Parmigiano-Reggiano cheese and cook, stirring, until thickened.
Stir in the parsley.

To assemble:
Drain the linguine, add to the sauce in the pan, and stir to coat.
Serve immediately on a platter with more grated Parmigiano-
Reggiano cheese.

2 pounds grass-fed ground beef

¼ cup maple stout beer

2 tablespoons olive oil

2 cups minced yellow onion

1 cup chopped red bell pepper

1 (15-ounce) can tomato sauce

¼ cup maple syrup

2 tablespoons tomato paste

1 tablespoon Sriracha hot sauce

2 teaspoons Worcestershire sauce

¼ cup water

Pepper and sea salt to taste

8 kaiser rolls, split

Serves 8

Maple Stout Sloppy Joes

GREEN SCENE, WALKER CHEF ERIN HAEFELE

This is not your mother's sloppy joe recipe! The smoky sweetness comes from maple syrup and maple stout beer (try Sugar Shack, a seasonal maple stout from Third Street Brewhouse in Cold Spring). The Green Scene market and deli is an oasis of healthy food near Leech Lake in the Chippewa National Forest.

In a large skillet, brown the ground beef until cooked through, then remove to a bowl. Deglaze the pan with the beer and add this to the beef in the bowl.

Add the olive oil to the pan and sauté the onion until translucent. Add the red pepper and sauté for another 3 or 4 minutes. Add the tomato sauce, maple syrup, tomato paste, hot sauce, and Worcestershire. Cook until bubbly and return the ground beef to the pan. Stir in the water and add salt and pepper to taste.

Spoon the sloppy joe mixture onto the kaiser rolls and serve immediately.

Pumpkin jam

1 medium (1½- to 2-pound)
    pie pumpkin

½ to 1 cup sugar, depending
    on the weight of the pumpkin

1 cinnamon stick

2 pods star anise

1 bay leaf

¼ cup cider vinegar

¼ cup water

Salt to taste

Pepito ancho butter

1 dried ancho chile

2 cups hot water

½ to 1 cup reserved pumpkin seeds

½ cup peanut oil

1 tablespoon maple syrup

Salt to taste

8 slices whole wheat bread

Makes 4 sandwiches

Pepito Ancho Butter and Pumpkin Jam Sandwiches

LAKE AVENUE RESTAURANT, DULUTH   ❧   CHEF TONY BERAN

Two tasty spreads made from one pumpkin make a simple sandwich special. At Lake Avenue, they serve these with Lake Superior Trout and Pumpkin Chowder (see the recipe in the Soups and Stews section, page 70). These spreads also work well as fun condiments to serve with cheeses, crackers, and crudité. For sandwiches, try the multigrain bread from Rustica Bakery.

For the pumpkin jam:
Cut the pumpkin in half and scoop out the seeds. Reserve the seeds. Using a vegetable peeler or paring knife, remove the tough skin.

Roughly dice the pumpkin flesh and weigh it (so you'll know how much sugar to use). Place the pumpkin in a heavy-bottomed pot. Add sugar equal to one-third the weight of the diced pumpkin (for example, 12 ounces of pumpkin will need 4 ounces—½ cup plus 1 tablespoon—of sugar). Add the cinnamon stick, star anise, bay leaf, vinegar, and water and simmer over low heat. Continue to cook, stirring frequently with a rubber spatula to scrape the bottom and sides of the pot.

Once the pumpkin begins to soften, mash with a potato masher or fork and cook until it is the consistency of thick applesauce. Remove from heat, let cool, and remove the cinnamon stick, anise pods, and bay leaf. Add salt to taste.

For the pepito ancho butter:
Remove the stem and seeds from the ancho chile. Tear the chile into small pieces, place in a small bowl, and cover with the hot water to soak for 30 minutes.

Meanwhile, place the pumpkin seeds in a small pot and barely cover with the peanut oil. Place on low heat and cook, stirring occasionally, until the seeds turn golden brown, about 30 minutes. Strain the seeds from the oil and reserve both.

Drain the water off the chile and add the chile pieces to the bowl of a food processor along with the roasted pumpkin seeds, maple syrup, and 1 tablespoon of the reserved peanut oil. Process for 4 minutes, occasionally scraping the sides of the bowl with a rubber spatula. Add more peanut oil, 1 tablespoon at a time, until the mixture reaches a creamy, spreadable consistency. Season to taste with salt and more maple syrup if desired.

To assemble:
Toast the bread slices. For each sandwich, spread pumpkin jam on one slice of bread and pepito ancho butter on another and combine.

Sesame basil pesto

2 cups packed basil

¼ cup sesame seeds, toasted

2 cloves garlic

⅔ cup extra virgin olive oil

1 teaspoon toasted sesame oil

1 teaspoon gochugaru
(Korean coarse-ground
chili flakes)

½ cup grated Parmesan cheese

Salt and pepper to taste

Pork loin katsu

1 ½ pounds center-cut pork loin

1 cup buttermilk

1 large egg

½ teaspoon salt

¼ cup flour

½ cup crushed saltine crackers

½ cup panko bread crumbs

1 ½ cups soybean oil or other
high-heat oil

Fingerling potato confit

8 ounces fingerling potatoes,
skin on

2 cups soybean oil or other
high-heat oil

Salt to taste

2 ounces Grana Padano or
Parmesan cheese, shaved

Pork Loin Katsu with Sesame Basil Pesto and Fingerling Potato Confit

THE RABBIT HOLE, MINNEAPOLIS   &   CHEF THOMAS KIM

Just as the food at The Rabbit Hole isn't "Americanized" Korean food, owners Thomas and Kat Kim are not "Americanized" Koreans. "We are Korean Americans and the Rabbit Hole is who we are," says Chef Kim. It couldn't be expressed more perfectly than in this comforting meat and potatoes dish that feels right at home in Minnesota with flavors that feed a free spirit.

For the sesame basil pesto:

In a food processor, blend the basil, sesame seeds, and garlic as you slowly drizzle in the olive oil. Mix until smooth and then add the sesame oil, gochugaru, Parmesan cheese, salt, and pepper. Blend to the desired consistency, taste, and adjust flavors. Refrigerate until ready to serve.

For the pork loin katsu:

Trim the fat from the pork loin and cut into 6–ounce portions. Pound the pork loin portions flat with a meat mallet or a small sauté pan to ½ inch thick. In a bowl, whisk together the buttermilk, egg, salt, and flour. Add the pork to the buttermilk marinade and refrigerate for a minimum of 6 hours or up to 1 day.

Mix the cracker crumbs with the panko in a shallow bowl. Coat the marinated pork with the crumbs and let rest at room temperature for 1 hour. Heat the soybean oil in a deep, heavy skillet to 345 degrees. Fry the pork until golden brown and keep warm until ready to serve.

For the fingerling potato confit:

Clean the fingerling potatoes. In a medium pan, heat the oil to 200 degrees, add the potatoes, and cook for 25 minutes. Hold in the oil until ready to serve.

1 pinch gaenip (Korean perilla leaf) or Thai basil or red shiso leaf, for garnish

Serves 4

To assemble:

When ready to serve, drop the potatoes into a saucepan with oil heated to 325 degrees. Cook for 4 to 5 minutes, then remove from heat. Drain off the oil and lightly season the potatoes with salt. Toss with the sesame basil pesto until coated and sprinkle with the cheese. Serve with the pork katsu and garnish with gaenip.

Dill mayonnaise

1 clove garlic

1 tablespoon kosher salt

2 egg yolks

4 tablespoons water

4 tablespoons fresh lemon juice

4 ounces fresh dill, roughly chopped

2 cups vegetable oil

Roasted chicken

1 clove garlic

1 teaspoon fresh thyme

2 tablespoons kosher salt

¼ cup vegetable oil

4 bone-in, skin-on chicken thighs

2 tablespoons butter

Coarse sea salt to taste

Clams and rapini

2 tablespoons vegetable oil

4 cloves garlic, sliced thin

Pinch red pepper flakes

1 cup dry white wine

12 clams, any variety

1 bunch rapini

¼ cup (½ stick) butter

½ lemon, juiced

Serves 4

Roasted Chicken Thighs with Clams, Rapini, and Dill Mayonnaise

HEYDAY, MINNEAPOLIS   &   CHEF JIM CHRISTIANSEN

Chef Christiansen, a Minnesota native, has been recognized by Food & Wine as one of the best new chefs of 2015. He says that when you make the clam sauce for this dish it should "taste like the ocean," an affinity likely sprouted during his time spent in the kitchen of Noma in Denmark. The sauce makes for an inspired pairing with the earthiness of the roasted chicken thighs.

For the dill mayonnaise:
In a blender, add the garlic, salt, egg yolks, water, lemon juice, and dill. Blend on high until a bright green emulsion forms, then set on mix and slowly add the oil until the mayonnaise thickens. Set aside until ready to plate.

For the roasted chicken:
Peel the garlic and chop, mixing in the thyme and salt. Rub each thigh in the garlic mix and refrigerate for at least an hour or up to 24 hours.

To roast the chicken, heat a large pan over high heat. Add the vegetable oil and place the chicken skin side down. Press to ensure even roasting of the skin. Reduce heat to medium and cook until the skin is crispy, about 10 minutes.

Add the butter, let it brown, then turn off heat, flip the chicken over, and let rest in the pan until ready to plate.

For the clams and rapini:
In a large pan, heat the vegetable oil and sliced garlic. Cook the garlic until lightly brown, no darker. Add the red pepper flakes, wine, and clams and continue cooking until most of the liquid has evaporated.

Trim the stems off the rapini. Add the butter, rapini, and lemon juice and cover with a lid to steam open the clams, about 2 minutes. Once the clams open, continue reducing the sauce until it turns glossy. Season as needed.

To assemble:
Season the chicken with coarse sea salt and plate. Divide the rapini and clams, with pan sauce, between four plates. Add a spoonful of dill mayonnaise and serve immediately.

1 (10-inch) pie crust, unbaked

4 large free-range eggs

2 cups sour cream

½ cup finely chopped onion

½ teaspoon salt

1 tablespoon chopped fresh
    or dried dill

1 ½ cups shredded Cheddar
    cheese, divided

1 pound baked or smoked
    sockeye salmon, deboned,
    skinned, and flaked

1 lemon, cut into wedges

Serves 6 to 8

Salmon and Cheddar Quiche

AMBOY COTTAGE CAFE, AMBOY   ❧   LISA LINDBERG

*Truly a hidden gem in southwestern rural Minnesota, the Amboy Cottage
Cafe offers food made from scratch and featuring local ingredients (like
Fini Cheddar from the Caves of Faribault dairy). It is a charming place
for people to gather, sharing stories and good food. Enjoy this savory
dish warm or chilled.*

Preheat the oven to 350 degrees.

Line a pie plate with the pie crust and crimp the edges as desired. In
a medium bowl, beat together the eggs and sour cream. Stir in the
onion, salt, dill, and all but ¼ cup
of the cheese. Fold in the salmon and then turn the mixture into the
pie crust. Sprinkle with the reserved ¼ cup of cheese. Bake until set,
45 to 50 minutes.

Allow to cool 10 minutes before serving. Serve with lemon wedges.

Seared duck breast

4 (6- to 8-ounce) duck breasts,
  skin-on, boneless

Kosher salt and pepper

2 tablespoons olive oil

Fingerling sweet potato coins

8 each fingerling sweet potatoes,
  roasted 30 minutes
  at 250 degrees

2 tablespoons olive oil

½ cup rendered duck fat

Haricots verts

8 ounces haricots verts
  (slender green beans)

1 tablespoon butter

1 tablespoon water

Salt and pepper

Green oil

½ pound fresh Italian parsley

½ cup olive oil

½ teaspoon kosher salt

Seared Duck Breast and Amarena Cherries

NEW SCENIC CAFÉ, DULUTH   &   CHEF SCOTT GRADEN

The New Scenic Café is known for gorgeous plate presentations and quality ingredients. Special elements in this recipe, like the amarena cherry syrup and the green oil, are fun things to play chef with at home. Look for jarred amarena cherries at your local gourmet shop. Chef Graden teaches us the secret for crispy duck skin in this recipe.

For the seared duck breast:
Season the duck breasts with the kosher salt and black pepper on both sides. Pour the olive oil into a large, heavy sauté pan to coat the bottom. Lay the duck breasts in the pan, skin side down, and place the pan over medium–low heat, cooking the skin slowly so the fat renders out of the duck breast. Move the breasts around every few minutes, checking to see that they are cooking evenly. Cook until the skin is golden brown and crisp, 15 to 20 minutes. Flip the duck breasts over and cook them on the other side for about 2 minutes more. Remove from the pan and set them on a paper towel to rest for about 5 minutes. Reserve the rendered duck fat.

For the fingerling sweet potato coins:
Slice the roasted sweet potatoes into thin discs. Heat the olive oil and rendered duck fat in a large sauté pan until it begins to smoke. Add the fingerling coins and fry until golden brown on both sides. Remove from the fat and drain on paper towels.

For the haricots verts:
Place the haricots verts in a small pot with the butter, water, salt, and pepper and warm gently until al dente.

For the green oil:
Fill a medium pot with water and bring to a simmer. Fill a bowl with water and ice cubes. Blanch the parsley in the simmering water for 2 seconds, then plunge into the ice water. Squeeze out as much water as possible and then trim the leaves from the stems, discard

Presentation

4 black mission figs, quartered

12 amarena cherries

2 tablespoons amarena cherry
    syrup (from jar)

2 tablespoons green oil

4 sprigs fresh thyme

Serves 4

the stems, and rough chop the leaves. Place the parsley in a blender with the olive oil and kosher salt and puree until smooth and dark green. Line a fine-mesh strainer with damp cheesecloth, pour in the parsley puree, and allow to drain for an hour. Discard the solids and refrigerate the green oil.

For the presentation:
Slice the duck breasts thinly, skin side down, taking care not to cut all the way through the skin, so the breast fans like an accordion. Arrange the fingerling sweet potato coins on each plate and place the haricots verts alongside. Set the sliced duck breast across the beans, skin side down and fanned across. Arrange the figs and cherries on each plate and artfully drizzle the cherry syrup and green oil around the edge of the plate. Garnish with thyme sprigs.

Sommer Pasta

LA FERME, ALEXANDRIA
CHEF AND OWNER MATTHEW JENSEN

Good food comes down to a true and simple source: la ferme (the farm). Chef Jensen appreciates all the amazing local farmers who supply the restaurant, and this pasta dish celebrates the bounty of sommer (summer) in all its glory. La Ferme makes its pasta from scratch.

Bring a large pot of salted water to a boil and keep at a simmer until ready to cook the pasta. If using dried pasta, cook until al dente, drain, and reserve.

Melt the butter in a large sauté pan over medium heat, add the onions, and cook until translucent. Add the corn kernels and cook for 1 minute. Add the zucchini, summer squash, and garlic and cook until you can smell the garlic, about 30 seconds. Add the white wine and simmer until the wine is almost gone. Add the cream and return to a simmer.

Meanwhile, blanch the fresh pasta in the boiling water until it floats to the top. Drain the pasta and toss with the vegetables in cream. Add the tomato and tarragon just before serving.

1 pound fresh pasta,
    or ½ pound dry pasta

2 tablespoons butter

1 small onion, small dice

3 ears corn, kernels cut off cob

1 small zucchini, small dice

1 small yellow summer squash,
    small dice

2 cloves garlic, minced

¼ cup white wine

1 cup heavy cream

1 large garden tomato,
    seeded and small dice

1 tablespoon minced
    fresh tarragon

Serves 4

4 pounds bone-in beef short ribs

Salt and pepper to taste

3 tablespoons canola oil

½ cup rough-chopped carrots

1 cup chopped onion

½ cup chopped celery

3 cloves garlic, peeled and
    lightly smashed with a knife

3 sprigs fresh tarragon

1 pint Surly Bender beer

4 cups (1 quart) beef stock

3 bay leaves

Serves 4 to 6

Surly Bender Braised Short Ribs

INSULA RESTAURANT, ELY   &   CHEF DANIEL VOLLOM

It is a simple pleasure to slow-braise a dish like this on a lazy fall or winter weekend when it feels great to have the oven on and the smell is welcoming to all who come in from the cold. Surly Bender, an oatmeal brown ale, adds a nice element of earthy flavor to the short ribs.

Preheat the oven to 325 degrees.

Season the beef ribs with salt and pepper. Heat the oil in a Dutch oven or large, oven–safe saucepan and sear the beef on all sides to a caramel brown color. Remove the beef from the pan, add the carrots, onion, and celery and sauté until caramelized and dark brown in color. Add the garlic and tarragon and sauté for 2 minutes. Add the beer, beef stock, and bay leaves. Lay the beef ribs on top of the vegetables and liquid, cover, and braise until the meat is falling–off–the–bone tender, about 3½ hours.

& **Note:** *Any leftover braising liquid makes an amazing stock for beef barley soup or chili.*

Sweet crispy beef

1 teaspoon white pepper

3 tablespoons whiskey

2 tablespoons mushroom soy sauce
(Healthy Boy brand)

1 tablespoon oyster sauce
(Maekrua brand)

1½ teaspoons salt

5 tablespoons palm sugar

4 teaspoons toasted coriander
seeds, cracked and crushed

2 pounds beef sirloin steak or
flank steak, sliced ⅛ inch thick

3 cups vegetable oil

Nam pla prik (fish sauce with chiles and lime juice)

2 tablespoons fish sauce

3 tablespoons lime juice

2 cloves garlic, minced

6 Thai chiles, chopped

1 tablespoon toasted rice powder

1 tablespoon chopped
fresh cilantro

Pinch sugar

Serves 4 to 6

Sweet Crispy Beef with Coriander Seed (Nuea Dat Deow)

SEN YAI SEN LEK, MINNEAPOLIS
CHEF JOE HATCH-SURISOOK

Not unlike beef jerky, this dish is great paired with a nice local brew and becomes more of a meal than a snack when accompanied by sticky rice, green papaya salad (som tum), and fresh vegetables. (Look for som tum recipes online, or sign up for a Thai cooking class with Chef Hatch-Surisook at the Kitchen Window cooking school in Minneapolis.) For the marinade, 2 Gingers whiskey works well in this dish.

For the sweet crispy beef:
In a medium bowl, thoroughly combine the white pepper, whiskey, soy sauce, oyster sauce, salt, sugar, and coriander seeds and add the beef slices, coating well with the marinade. Cover and refrigerate for at least an hour.

Preheat the oven to 150 degrees or use a food dehydrator. Drain the beef from the marinade and pat dry. Arrange the beef on an oven-safe rack in a single layer and dry the beef for 1½ to 2 hours.

When the beef has dried, heat the oil in a large pan to 350 degrees. Working in batches, fry the beef for 2 to 3 minutes. Remove with a slotted spoon and drain on paper towels.

For the nam pla prik:
In a bowl, combine the fish sauce and lime juice, then add the garlic, Thai chiles, rice powder, cilantro, and sugar. Stir to mix well.

Serve the beef with sticky rice and fresh vegetables, with bowls of nam pla prik for dipping the beef.

1½-pound venison tenderloin, cut into 4 portions

1 cup miso paste (all-natural imported Japanese miso)

4 large egg yolks

½ cup sake

½ cup sugar

4 tablespoons dashi (Japanese bonito stock)

⅛ cup dried, smoked bonito flakes

1 tablespoon raw sesame oil

Freshly ground white pepper

Healthy pinch sea salt

1 tablespoon grape seed oil

Serves 4

Venison Tenderloin with Miso Sauce

AZ CANTEEN, FOOD WORKS, BIZARRE FOODS, MINNEAPOLIS
CHEF ANDREW ZIMMERN

Chef Zimmern, a three-time James Beard Award-winning TV personality, chef, writer, and teacher, likes to serve venison with this sauce for its "incomparable sweet and salty qualities with deep umami bass notes." He also suggests roasted mushrooms to complete this plate.

Bring the venison to room temperature. Meanwhile, combine the miso, egg yolks, sake, sugar, dashi, and bonito flakes in the top chamber of a double boiler, or in a steel bowl set over simmering water. Over the slowly boiling water, whisk the mixture until the eggs set and the sauce thickens. The fermented proteins and acids prevent the eggs from curdling as long as you don't boil the water too hard. Use a food thermometer and cook the sauce until it reaches 165 degrees. This sauce can be made in advance and reheats well.

When the venison reaches room temperature, season it with the sesame oil, white pepper, and sea salt. Set a cast–iron skillet over medium heat for 5 minutes, then raise the heat to high, add a tablespoon of grape seed oil, and swirl. Carefully add the meat to the pan and sear to brown on one side. Flip and cook on the other side. For a 1½–inch-thick cut, cook for 3 to 4 minutes on each side.

Allow the meat to rest for 5 minutes. Slice and serve with the miso sauce and sautéed wild mushrooms.

Ginger-orange teriyaki sauce

⅔ cup soy sauce

¼ cup mirin (sweet rice wine)

⅓ cup maple syrup or brown sugar

1 tablespoon finely grated or minced fresh ginger root

2 tablespoons orange juice concentrate

Walleye with sesame crust

½ cup sesame seeds

2 tablespoons black sesame seeds (optional)

¼ cup cornmeal

¼ teaspoon salt

1 ¼ pounds skinless walleye fillets

5 tablespoons vegetable oil

Serves 4

Walleye with Sesame Crust and Ginger-Orange Teriyaki

SPOONRIVER, MINNEAPOLIS ❧ CHEF BRENDA LANGTON

Think outside the "shore lunch" package and try something new with walleye and other panfish. This teriyaki sauce is delicate enough to not overpower the flavor of the fish, and it makes plenty, so save leftover sauce to serve with vegetables, chicken, or steak.

For the ginger-orange teriyaki sauce:
Place the soy sauce, mirin, maple syrup, and ginger in a medium saucepan. Bring the mixture to a boil, then turn the heat to low and simmer until it reaches a syrupy consistency, about 20 minutes. Remove from heat and cool slightly before stirring in the orange juice concentrate.

For the walleye with sesame crust:
In a large bowl, stir together the sesame seeds, cornmeal, and salt. Dredge the fish fillets in the mixture to coat. Heat the oil in a large skillet over medium heat. Add the fish and sauté until golden brown on each side, 3 to 4 minutes per side.

Serve each piece drizzled with a tablespoon of ginger–orange teriyaki sauce.

❧ **Note:** *If you're fresh out of walleye, substitute any flaky white fish, such as cisco or lake whitefish.*

Desserts & Sweet Treats

Whiskey Honey Cake with Whiskey Whipped Cream Filling, p. 146

2 cups (about 2 medium) diced apple

2 tablespoons grated ginger root

2 tablespoons maple syrup

8 tablespoons (1 stick) butter, divided

1 loaf (14 ounces) ciabatta bread, cut into 1-inch cubes

3 cups whole milk

2 cups heavy cream, divided

2 whole eggs

4 egg yolks

1 cup brown sugar

1½ teaspoons vanilla extract

3 tablespoons turbinado sugar

Serves 10

Apple-Ginger Bread Pudding

THE NEW MIDWESTERN TABLE, PARK RAPIDS
CHEF AMY THIELEN

Chef Thielen calls for cooking the custard not until it reaches a certain temperature or is thick, but just long enough to "engage" the eggs and start them on the path to making a smooth custard. It's a small step that makes an enormous difference in the texture of the final pudding.

Preheat the oven to 350 degrees. Stir together the diced apples, ginger root, and maple syrup in a 9 x 13–inch baking pan. Roast in the oven, stirring occasionally, until tender, about 20 minutes. Spoon the apples from the pan into a bowl and rub the pan with 1 tablespoon of butter.

Place the remaining 7 tablespoons of butter in a small skillet and set over medium heat. Cook until the butter has browned and smells nutty; remove from heat. Toss the bread cubes with the brown butter to coat and add the roasted apples. Set aside while you prepare the custard.

Combine the milk and 1½ cups of the cream in a 2-quart saucepan over medium heat. Cook until bubbles form at the edges and then remove from heat. In a small bowl, whisk the whole eggs, yolks, and sugar until well combined. Gradually add the hot milk mixture to the eggs in a thin stream, whisking constantly. Pour the milk and egg mixture back into the pot and set over low heat. Cook, circling the bottom of the pot with a rubber spatula, until the cream thickens slightly and feels hot to the touch, about 5 minutes. Stir in the vanilla extract.

Pour the custard over the bread cubes and apples in the bowl, mix well to coat, then scrape out into the buttered 9 x 13–inch pan. Bake for 20 minutes, remove from the oven, and press lightly on the bread cubes to make sure they are all submerged in the custard. Sprinkle the top with the turbinado sugar and bake until golden brown and puffed, about 40 minutes. Serve warm with a drizzle of heavy cream, or chilled with lightly sweetened whipped cream.

Palisade Porter caramel sauce

1 cup Palisade Porter

½ cup brown sugar

¼ cup corn syrup

¼ cup (½ stick) butter

1 cup heavy cream

Pinch salt and pepper to taste

Maple-glazed bacon

2 slices thick-sliced bacon

2 tablespoons real maple syrup

Sundae

1 pint vanilla ice cream

½ cup Palisade Porter
   caramel sauce

Maple-glazed bacon pieces

Serves 4

Beer and Bacon Caramel Sundae

VOYAGEUR BREWING COMPANY, GRAND MARAIS
CHEF CHARLES CONROY

The taproom for the brewery faces magnificent Lake Superior, the source of the water with which the beer is made. For this dish, Palisade Porter adds depth to the silky caramel sauce, and the surprise element of the salty, smoky, sweet bacon pieces makes this sundae perfection!

For the Palisade Porter caramel sauce:
Preheat the oven to 375 degrees. In a medium saucepan over medium heat, simmer the porter until reduced by half, about 10 minutes. Remove from heat. In a separate saucepan, heat the brown sugar and corn syrup together until the brown sugar has dissolved. Stir in the beer reduction and bring to a boil. Gradually stir in the butter until it is fully incorporated. Bring this mixture to a boil and then remove from heat.

Stir in the heavy cream until the mixture is smooth and season with salt and pepper to taste. Set aside to cool.

For the maple-glazed bacon:
Chop the bacon slices into small pieces and toss in a small bowl with the maple syrup to coat. Line a small baking sheet with parchment paper and scatter the maple–coated bacon pieces over the paper in an even layer. Bake until the bacon is browned and crisp, 12 to 15 minutes. Remove the bacon from the oven and let cool.

For the sundae:
Scoop the ice cream into four dishes and top each with 2 table–spoons of caramel sauce. Sprinkle with the maple–glazed bacon. Store leftover caramel sauce in a covered container in the refrigerator.

Lemon-thyme shortbread crust

½ cup powdered sugar

1 ½ cups flour

¾ cup (1 ½ sticks) butter, chilled

Pinch salt

1 teaspoon finely chopped
lemon thyme

Cream cheese dough

4 ounces cream cheese,
room temperature

¼ cup (½ stick) butter

¼ cup powdered sugar

1 cup flour

Blueberry filling

½ cup sugar

2 tablespoons cornstarch

6 cups fresh or frozen blueberries

1 tablespoon finely chopped
fresh ginger root

1 egg, beaten with 1 tablespoon
water, to brush crust

Makes 16 bars

Blueberry Bars with Lemon-Thyme Shortbread Crust

ZOË BAKES AND *FIVE MINUTES A DAY* AUTHOR, MINNEAPOLIS
CHEF ZOË FRANÇOIS

Weaving the pastry lattice top is easy if you follow Chef François's steps described below. Chilling the lattice in its entirety keeps the pastry strips neat. And lemon thyme is the secret ingredient that will make these bars the hit of the bake sale!

Preheat the oven to 350 degrees. Butter a 9 x 9-inch baking pan.

For the lemon-thyme shortbread crust:
In the bowl of a food processor, combine the powdered sugar, flour, butter, salt, and lemon thyme and process until a dough forms. (Don't bother cleaning the food processor bowl as it will be used again for the cream cheese crust.) Press the shortbread dough into the prepared baking pan, cover with plastic wrap, and gently press the shortbread smooth with your hand. Remove the plastic wrap and bake on the middle rack in the oven until a light golden brown, about 20 minutes. Set the crust aside to cool.

For the cream cheese dough:
In the food processor bowl, mix the cream cheese, butter, and powdered sugar until smooth and then pulse in the flour until the dough comes to a soft ball. Shape the dough into a disc, wrap with plastic, and refrigerate for an hour.

For the blueberry filling:
In a small bowl, stir together the sugar and cornstarch. Place the blueberries and ginger in a saucepan and then add the sugar mix. Cook over low heat until the blueberries thicken and reduce by about half their volume. You should end up with 2½ cups of blueberry filling. Remove from heat and let cool.

To assemble:

On a well-floured surface, roll out the chilled cream cheese dough about ⅛ inch thick to form a 9-inch square. Use a pastry cutter or a knife to cut ½-inch-wide strips. To weave the lattice crust, arrange half of the strips running left to right on a sheet of parchment about ½ inch apart. One strip at a time, lift the right end of every other strip and fold it over on itself from the midpoint. Lay a strip of the remaining dough perpendicularly on top of the strips that are lying flat on the parchment, then fold down the strips that were folded up. Next, fold up the opposite left-to-right strips on the parchment and add another pastry strip. Repeat these steps until you reach the right-hand edge of the pastry. Then repeat this process working from the left until all strips are woven into the lattice.

Place the parchment with the lattice on a rack in the freezer to firm it up. Heat the oven to 350 degrees. Spread the blueberry filling on top of the baked shortbread layer and, when the lattice is firm, gently slide it off the parchment onto the blueberry layer, using a spatula to guide it onto the top of the pan. Brush the lattice with egg wash and bake the bars until the crust is golden and the filling is bubbly, 35 to 40 minutes. Allow the bars to cool completely before cutting into squares.

1 tablespoon popcorn kernels

1 teaspoon vegetable oil

3 tablespoons salted butter, melted

2 pinches sea salt

3 cups whole milk

1 cup heavy cream

12 egg yolks

1¼ cups sugar

1 cup caramel corn, for garnish

Serves 8

Buttered Popcorn Pot de Crème

VICTORY 44, MINNEAPOLIS   ❧   CHEF ERICK HARCEY

Minneapolis is full of comfortable neighborhood restaurants like Victory 44, beloved by locals and far-roaming foodies alike. The familiar flavor of popcorn in a silky, creamy custard conjures old memories while creating new ones.

Preheat the oven to 325 degrees.

In a large, lidded pot over medium-high heat, pop the popcorn kernels in the vegetable oil and toss with the butter and salt.

Heat the milk and cream in a large saucepan over medium heat and add the popped corn. Bring to a simmer and then turn off the heat and let the popcorn steep in the cream for 10 minutes. In a large bowl, whisk together the egg yolks and sugar until creamy (this may take 10 minutes). Strain the popcorn-infused cream through a fine strainer into the yolk mixture, stirring well to blend. Add another pinch of salt.

Pour the mixture into eight ramekins and place them in a deep-sided baking pan. Pour hot water into the baking pan so it reaches halfway up the sides of the ramekins. Bake for 45 minutes. Gently remove the ramekins from the water and refrigerate overnight. Garnish with caramel corn before serving.

3 cups flour

1 tablespoon baking powder

¼ cup sugar

¼ teaspoon salt

1½ cups heavy cream

¼ cup honey

½ cup dried cherries,
    coarsely chopped

½ cup toasted pecan pieces,
    coarsely chopped

Coarse sugar, for sprinkling
    on top (optional)

Makes 8 scones

Cherry Pecan Scones

PATISSERIE 46, MINNEAPOLIS   CHEF JOHN KRAUS

The alluring smell of baked goods is matched by the swoon-worthy treats that fill the pastry case at Patisserie 46. You'll find it tucked into the Kingfield neighborhood of South Minneapolis with a down-to-earth vibe where people gather for conversation, fine coffee, and pastry. Bake up these inviting scones when friends come to call.

Preheat the oven to 375 degrees. Line a baking sheet with parchment paper.

In a large bowl, sift together the flour and baking powder. Whisk in the sugar and salt. In a separate bowl, stir together the cream and honey and add to the flour, mixing gently to just moisten the dry ingredients; do not over-mix. Fold in the dried cherries and pecans.

Gently pat the scone dough onto a floured board and cut with a circle cutter (or cut into eight triangles with a sharp knife). Transfer the scones to the lined baking sheet, allowing at least an inch around each scone for spreading. Sprinkle the scones with coarse sugar, if desired. Bake until golden brown, 20 to 25 minutes.

Chestnut crème brûlée

2 cups heavy cream

¼ cup brown sugar

½ bay leaf

1-inch piece of vanilla bean, split with seeds scraped out

¼ pound chestnut meat, roasted

5 egg yolks

3 tablespoons sugar

1 tablespoon Madeira wine

Cognac-marinated prunes

⅔ cup water

3 tablespoons sugar

3 ounces cognac or brandy

1 clove

½ star anise

½ cinnamon stick

⅓ cup prunes, halved

Serves 6

Chestnut Crème Brûlée with Cognac-Marinated Prunes

THE KENWOOD RESTAURANT, MINNEAPOLIS
CHEF DON SAUNDERS

Prunes may not be flashy, bright, and brazen like cherries, but neither do they lack sex appeal, especially when soaked in spice-scented cognac syrup. I wouldn't kick this silky custard out of bed for eating crackers, either.

For the chestnut crème brûlée:
Preheat the oven to 325 degrees. In a medium saucepan, combine the cream, brown sugar, bay leaf, vanilla bean, and chestnuts. Simmer for 15 minutes. Remove from heat and take out the bay leaf and vanilla bean. Pour into a blender and blend until smooth.

In a large bowl, whisk together the egg yolks, sugar, and Madeira. Gradually pour the hot chestnut and cream mixture into the egg yolks, whisking constantly. Pour this mixture into six ramekins. Place ramekins in a large, deep-sided baking pan and fill the pan with hot water halfway up the sides of the ramekins.

Bake until the custard is almost set and the center is not wobbly when you shake it gently, 20 to 25 minutes. Remove from the oven and refrigerate.

For the cognac-marinated prunes:
Combine the water, sugar, cognac, and spices in a saucepan. Bring to a boil and cook until reduced by half. Pour over the prunes in a bowl, cover, and refrigerate.

To assemble:
When the custards have cooled thoroughly, sprinkle a thin layer of sugar over each crème brûlée. Using a small kitchen torch, caramelize the sugar to an amber color. If you do not have a kitchen torch, broil them in an oven or toaster oven, watching closely to avoid scorching. Let rest for 2 minutes to allow the caramelized sugar to set up. Top with a dollop of the marinated prunes and serve.

1/4 cup sunflower oil

1/2 cup honey

1 egg, lightly beaten

1 cup orange juice

2 tablespoons grated orange zest

2 cups whole wheat pastry flour

2 teaspoons baking powder

1/2 teaspoon baking soda

1/2 teaspoon salt

1/2 cup chopped walnuts
    or pecans

1 cup fresh or frozen cranberries,
    coarsely chopped

Makes 1 loaf

Cranberry-Orange Bread

SPOONRIVER, MINNEAPOLIS   ❦   CHEF BRENDA LANGTON

When the weather turns cool and cranberries are in season, Minnesotans are inclined to turn on their ovens and bake. This moist quick bread is wholesome enough for everyday and pretty enough for company.

Preheat the oven to 350 degrees (*see Note*). Oil a loaf pan and dust lightly with flour.

In a large bowl, whisk the oil and honey together until the mixture is light and creamy. Add the egg, orange juice, and zest, beating until well mixed. In a separate bowl, combine the flour, baking powder, baking soda, and salt. Stir the dry ingredients into the wet ingredients until just combined. Stir in the nuts and cranberries.

Pour the batter into the prepared loaf pan. Bake until a toothpick inserted into the middle comes out clean, 50 to 60 minutes. Allow the bread to cool for 10 minutes before turning out onto a cooling rack. Cool the bread completely before slicing.

❦ **Note:** *If using a glass loaf pan, bake at 325 degrees.*

Ginger Ginger Cookies

HONEY AND RYE BAKEHOUSE, ST. LOUIS PARK
CHEF AND OWNER ANNE ANDRUS AND BAKER SARAH STONE

Ginger stars in these cookies in two forms, ground and candied, doubling their flavor and appeal. They are satisfyingly crisp on the outside and oh-my-gosh chewy on the inside.

3 cups flour

2 teaspoons baking soda

1 teaspoon salt

2 teaspoons ground ginger

1 teaspoon ground cloves

1 teaspoon ground cinnamon

1 teaspoon ground nutmeg

Pinch allspice

1 cup (2 sticks) butter,
    room temperature

1 ⅓ cups brown sugar,
    firmly packed

1 egg

½ cup molasses

1 ½ teaspoons vanilla extract

¼ cup finely chopped crystallized
    ginger root

½ cup coarse decorator's sugar

Makes about 2 dozen cookies

Preheat the oven to 350 degrees. Line two baking sheets with parchment paper.

In a medium bowl, whisk together the flour, soda, salt, and spices. In a stand mixer bowl, cream the butter and brown sugar together until pale and light, about 1 minute on medium speed. (If using a handheld mixer, this will take a few more minutes.) Add the egg, molasses, and vanilla to the mixer bowl. Mix with a paddle attachment on low speed until incorporated, about 1 minute.

Add the dry ingredients and crystallized ginger until just blended, being careful not to over-mix.

Form the dough into golf-ball-size balls and roll in the coarse sugar. Arrange on the parchment-lined baking sheets, allowing an inch on each side for cookies to spread. Bake until cookies appear crackled on top, 10 to 12 minutes. Allow to cool 5 to 10 minutes on the baking sheet before transferring to a cooling rack.

10 ounces fresh chèvre

5 whole Medjool dates,
    pitted and coarsely chopped

2 tablespoons light and floral honey

½ cup finely ground pistachios

Makes 12 truffles

Goat Cheese, Honey, Date, and Pistachio Truffles

THE WEDGE & WHEEL, STILLWATER
CHEF AND OWNER CHRIS KOHTZ

Located just yards from the St. Croix River, The Wedge & Wheel is a crossroads between the dairy traditions of Wisconsin and the grains and farms of Minnesota. This award-winning recipe would be lovely paired with an off-dry Riesling or sparkling moscato to keep up with the sweetness of the truffle.

In a bowl, use a wooden spoon or your hands to mix the chèvre, dates, and honey until smooth. Scoop by tablespoonful and roll into balls with your hands. Lightly roll each ball in the ground pistachios and then roll again lightly to press the nuts into the truffle. Refrigerate until ready to serve.

❧ **Note:** *Enjoy these truffles with Minnesota-made ingredients, such as chèvre from Stickney Hill Dairy in Kimball and basswood honey from Ames Farm in Delano.*

Cheesecake crust

10 tablespoons butter,
    melted and divided

2½ cups graham cracker crumbs

1½ tablespoons honey

Honey-vanilla cheesecake filling

20 ounces cream cheese, softened

1 cup plus 2 tablespoons
    sour cream

½ cup sugar

1 tablespoon vanilla extract

2 whole eggs

3 egg yolks

⅓ cup heavy cream

¼ cup honey

Blueberry caramel sauce

2 cups fresh blueberries

5 tablespoons water

Pinch kosher salt

¼ cup honey

1¼ cups sugar

2 teaspoons fresh lemon juice

Honey-Vanilla Cheesecake with Blueberry Caramel Sauce

INSULA RESTAURANT, ELY   ⌘   CHEF DANIEL VOLLOM

Insula is a large, island-studded lake in the Boundary Waters Canoe Area. If that is your destination, you may want to fortify yourself with some scrumptious cheesecake before you subsist on dehydrated meals. Visit Ely in late July for the Blueberry Festival to sample this and other blueberry treats.

For the cheesecake crust:
Preheat the oven to 300 degrees. Brush an 8-inch springform pan with 2 tablespoons of the melted butter. Line the bottom and the sides of the pan with parchment paper.

In a medium bowl, mix the graham cracker crumbs with the remaining butter and the honey until smooth. Press two-thirds of the crumb mixture into the bottom of the springform pan and spread out the remaining third in another baking pan (these crumbs will be for pressing into the cheesecake once it is baked). Bake both pans for 10 minutes. Remove from the oven and wrap the outside of the springform pan with aluminum foil.

Lower the oven temperature to 250 degrees. Fill a 9 x 13-inch baking pan with warm water so that the water comes halfway up the side of the springform pan.

For the honey-vanilla cheesecake filling:
Beat the cream cheese in a mixer for 20 seconds until smooth. Add the sour cream and beat for 15 seconds, scraping down the sides of the bowl between mixing. Add the sugar and beat on low for 15 seconds. Increase the speed to medium and beat for 15 seconds more. Scrape the bowl and beat another few seconds until smooth.

(continued on page 136)

Candied lemon zest

Peel of 2 lemons

1 1/3 cups sugar

1 tablespoon honey

1/2 cup water

1/2 cup sugar

Serves 12 to 16

In a separate bowl, combine the vanilla, eggs, yolks, and cream. Beat half of the egg mixture into the cream cheese mixture until smooth, then scrape down the sides and add the remaining egg mixture. Beat in the honey and mix until thoroughly combined, 10 to 20 seconds. Pour into the baked crust and smooth the top.

Place the pan into the water bath and bake until set, 60 to 75 minutes. Turn off the oven and open the door a moment to drop the temperature, then close and leave the cake in the oven for 1 hour. Remove the cheesecake from the oven and water bath and remove the foil. Cool for at least 15 minutes and then chill in the refrigerator for at least 6 hours. When the cheesecake has thoroughly chilled, remove the side of the springform pan and press the reserved graham cracker crumbs into the sides of the cheesecake. Keep chilled.

For the blueberry caramel sauce:
Combine the blueberries, 1 tablespoon of water, and salt in a saucepan. Over low heat, lightly mash the berries and stir for 4 minutes, then stir in the honey and remove from heat.

In another saucepan, combine the sugar, 4 tablespoons of water, and lemon juice. Stir over low heat until the sugar melts. Raise the heat to medium–high and boil without stirring until the liquid is a golden amber color, about 9 minutes, and then remove from heat. Stir in the blueberry mixture with a rubber spatula, stirring until mostly combined. Let stand 5 minutes and then mix again until smooth. Let cool.

For the candied lemon zest:
Peel the lemons with a peeler and cut the zest into thin strips. Blanch the zest strips in boiling water for about 1 minute. Remove and plunge into cold water to cool.

In a saucepan, bring the sugar, honey, and water to a boil. Reduce the heat to a simmer, add the lemon zest, and simmer until translucent, 12 to 20 minutes, depending on the thickness of the zests. Pick the strips out of the syrup and drop onto parchment paper to drain, keeping the strands separate so they don't stick together. When the strips are cool, roll in sugar and set on clean parchment paper.

Serve the cheesecake slices drizzled with blueberry caramel sauce and garnished with candied lemon zest.

Mascarpone no-bake cheesecake

5 gelatin sheets

⅔ cup sugar

8 ounces cream cheese

8 ounces mascarpone

¼ cup sour cream

1½ teaspoons vanilla extract

1 teaspoon orange zest

1½ cups cream

Candied orange zest

5 oranges, orange rind (no pith) and juiced

¾ cup water

¾ cup sugar

Chocolate-graham soil

½ cup crushed graham crackers

2 tablespoons butter, melted

½ cup chocolate chips, chilled

1 tablespoon Wondra flour

1½ teaspoons sea salt, preferably Maldon

Makes 6 small cheesecakes

Mascarpone No-Bake Cheesecake with Chocolate-Graham Soil

TONGUE IN CHEEK, ST. PAUL ✎ CHEF LEONARD ANDERSON

Present this chic, do-ahead dessert at your next dinner party without breaking a sweat. This ethereal cheesecake is scented with orange zest and grounded by the chocolate soil (a culinary term for "crumbs").

For the mascarpone no-bake cheesecake:
Set the gelatin sheets to soak in a bowl of cold water.

In a large bowl, cream together the sugar, cream cheese, mascarpone, sour cream, vanilla, and orange zest until smooth. In a saucepan over medium heat, bring the cream almost to a simmer, remove from heat, and whisk in the gelatin sheets. Pour the cream and gelatin into the cream cheese base and stir to combine. Portion into small custard cups or silicone molds and refrigerate overnight to set.

For the candied orange zest:
Peel the oranges, keeping the rind (without the pith) as intact as possible. Tightly roll each rind and slice perpendicular to the roll (chiffonade) to obtain long, slender strips. In a medium saucepan, bring the water and sugar to a simmer to form a simple syrup, then remove from heat and let cool. Simmer the chiffonade rind in the simple syrup until soft. Refrigerate until ready to assemble the dessert.

For the chocolate-graham soil:
Preheat the oven to 350 degrees. Chill the chocolate chips in the refrigerator. In a food processor, pulse the graham crackers and add

(continued on page 138)

the melted butter. Pulse until the mixture resembles wet sand, then spread it out onto parchment paper on a sheet tray. Bake until fragrant, about 5 minutes. Remove the graham crumbs from the oven and cool. Pulse again in the food processor with the cold chocolate chips, Wondra flour, and sea salt.

To assemble:
Dip the cheesecake cups or molds in warm water to release and invert the cakes onto serving plates. Scatter the chocolate soil on the side and top the cheesecake with the candied orange zest. Enjoy!

Molten Chocolate Cakes with Beer Ice Cream

LA FERME, ALEXANDRIA
CHEF AND OWNER MATTHEW JENSEN

The Homer Simpson in everyone should be groaning about now. Mmmmm . . . beer and molten chocolate. Choose a beer that isn't too bitter, since the beer is reduced to a syrup for making the ice cream. We used Bent Paddle Black Ale from Duluth.

Beer ice cream

1 pint (2 cups) dark beer, stout or porter

2 tablespoons maple syrup

¾ cup whole milk

1 cup heavy cream

5 large egg yolks

⅓ cup sugar

Molten chocolate cakes

¾ cup butter plus 2 tablespoons for buttering custard cups

½ cup sugar plus 2 tablespoons for dusting custard cups

8 ounces bittersweet chocolate, chopped

3 large whole eggs

3 large egg yolks

Serves 6

For the beer ice cream:
In a saucepan over low heat, reduce the beer to about ¼ cup. Add the maple syrup. In a separate pan, scald the milk and cream, then add to the syrup. Remove from heat.

In a large bowl, whisk together the five egg yolks and ⅓ cup sugar. Add a little of the hot cream mixture to the egg and sugar mixture and mix well. Gradually add the remaining cream to the yolks, mix well, and return the mixture to the pan and whisk constantly over low heat until it reaches 170 degrees. Strain through a fine sieve, cool completely, and refrigerate for at least 2 hours. When the custard is completely chilled, churn in an ice cream maker until it reaches the consistency of soft-serve ice cream. Store in the freezer until ready to use.

For the molten chocolate cakes:
Generously butter six custard cups (4- to 6-ounce capacity) or soufflé dishes with 2 tablespoons of butter and sprinkle with 2 tablespoons of sugar. Melt the chocolate and butter together in a heavy saucepan over low heat, stirring until smooth, then remove from heat.

In a large bowl, beat the whole eggs and the three egg yolks with ½ cup of sugar until thick and pale yellow, about 8 minutes. Fold one third of the warm chocolate mixture into the eggs, and then gradually fold in the remaining chocolate. Divide the batter evenly among the soufflé cups, cover with plastic wrap, and refrigerate. These can be made a week ahead of serving. When ready to serve, bake in a preheated 350-degree oven for 8 to 10 minutes on the middle rack. Serve in the dish with a scoop of beer ice cream.

Tart shell

1 ½ cups pastry flour
   or all-purpose flour

¼ teaspoon baking powder

½ cup (1 stick) butter, chilled,
   cut into small pieces

¼ teaspoon salt

½ cup sugar

3 egg yolks

Frangipane cream

5 ½ tablespoons butter, softened

⅓ cup sugar

Scant 1 cup (3 ounces) ground
   almond flour

2 eggs, room temperature

2 tablespoons heavy cream

1 teaspoon vanilla extract

2 teaspoons rum

2 large or 4 small plums

¼ cup sliced almonds

Serves 6 to 8

Plum Frangipane Tart

PATISSERIE 46, MINNEAPOLIS   ❧   CHEF JOHN KRAUS

When you are lucky enough to find some Minnesota-grown plums, you'll want to eat as many as you can fresh, then use the rest to bake this tart. Frangipane sounds like something from a fancy pastry shop, but the almond-based custard is simple enough to make at home. Ålander rum from Fär North Spirits is particularly tasty in the frangipane.

For the tart shell:
Combine the flour, baking powder, and cold butter in the bowl of an electric mixer with a paddle attachment. Mix until it is the consistency of wet sand. Blend in the salt and sugar. Add the egg yolks and mix until just coming together. Press the dough together to form a disc, wrap in plastic wrap, and refrigerate for at least 2 hours.

Preheat the oven to 325 degrees. Roll the chilled dough out on a floured board to ⅛ inch thick and press into an 8-inch tart pan. Cover the tart shell with aluminum foil held down by baking weights or dried beans and bake until lightly golden, about 25 minutes. Let the shell cool completely before filling.

For the frangipane cream:
In a medium bowl, cream together the butter and sugar, then add the almond flour, eggs, cream, vanilla, and rum, in that order. When the filling is smooth, refrigerate to chill well.

To assemble:
Pit the plums and cut into ½-inch slices. Pipe or spread a ½-inch layer of the frangipane cream in the base of the tart shell and arrange the plum slices on top. Sprinkle the tart with the sliced almonds and bake at 325 degrees until the custard is set and the almonds are golden brown, 35 to 40 minutes. Cool in the tart pan for at least 30 minutes before removing from the pan.

❧ *Note: If plums are unavailable, substitute nectarines, cherries, or other stone fruit.*

Raspberry filling

1 ½ cups fresh raspberries

3 tablespoons sugar

1 tablespoon cornstarch

1 teaspoon freshly grated
lemon zest

Galette crust

1 ¼ cups flour

Pinch kosher salt

2 teaspoons sugar

½ cup (1 stick) butter, chilled,
cut into pieces

1 large egg

1 teaspoon cold water

Serves 6

Raspberry Galette

BONICELLI KITCHEN, NORTHEAST MINNEAPOLIS
CHEF AND OWNER LAURA BONICELLI

*Carefree summer days when raspberries are abundant call for this rustic
tart—no pie plate needed! Chef Bonicelli likes to serve this with a scoop
of vanilla bean gelato.*

For the raspberry filling:
In a medium bowl, combine the raspberries with the sugar, cornstarch,
and lemon zest. Stir just enough to coat without mashing the berries.

For the galette crust:
In a food processor fitted with a metal blade, combine the flour, salt,
sugar, and butter. Pulse the processor until the butter is incorporated
in pea-size pieces. Combine the egg and water and add to the processor while running. Once a dough forms, stop the processor. Gather
the dough into a ball, press into a disc, and wrap in plastic wrap.
Refrigerate for 1 hour.

Preheat the oven to 400 degrees. Flatten the dough slightly and roll
out on a floured board to ¼-inch thick. Don't worry if the edges
seem rough; that is part of the look of the tart. Transfer the dough
to a parchment-lined baking sheet. Fill the center of the tart dough
with the raspberry filling to within 2 inches of the edge. Fold the
sides of the tart up over the edge of the filling.

Bake until the tart is golden brown and the filling is bubbly, about
30 minutes. Cool for at least 15 minutes before cutting and serving.

4 cups peeled (peels reserved) and chopped rhubarb

1 sprig fresh rosemary

1 cup sugar, or more if desired

Bittercube Jamaican #1 bitters to taste

Makes about 2¼ cups

Rosemary Rhubarb Jam

KITCHEN IN THE MARKET, MINNEAPOLIS   ❧   MOLLY HERRMANN

Chef Herrmann offers fun classes like Psychic Suppers, Wine O'Clock, and Chef's Night Off, which often end up in a spontaneous karaoke party. This jam has unexpected savory elements of Bittercube Jamaican #1 bitters and fresh rosemary, and it tastes good on pretty much anything it is dolloped on—scones, ice cream, cheeses, pork belly, or just a spoon!

Place the rhubarb peels and rosemary in a piece of cheesecloth and tie into a bundle. Place in a nonreactive saucepan. Add the rhubarb and sugar on top. Cook over medium heat, stirring and skimming foam occasionally, until the rhubarb is mostly broken down and no longer frothy. Add more sugar if desired. Remove the cheesecloth and squeeze the juice into the jam. Skim off any remaining foam. Add the bitters, stir, and taste.

Process in canning jars or store in clean lidded jars in the refrigerator. If you don't eat it all right away, refrigerated leftovers should last at least 4 months.

Surly Furious chocolate cake

½ pint (1 cup) Surly Furious beer
(reserve remainder for ganache)

1 cup (2 sticks) butter

1 cup cocoa powder

2½ cups sugar

2 eggs, beaten

6 ounces sour cream

2¼ cups cake flour

1½ teaspoons baking soda

¾ teaspoon salt

Ganache

8 ounces bittersweet chocolate,
chopped

½ pint (1 cup) Surly Furious beer

1 cup heavy cream

Serves 16

Surly Furious Chocolate Bundt Cake

SALTY TART, MINNEAPOLIS ❧ CHEF MICHELLE GAYER

This recipe celebrates the decadent flavors of Chef Gayer's Surly Furious Chocolate Cake but in the iconic shape of the bundt. Fun fact: The birthplace of the bundt pan is right here in Minnesota, made by the Nordic Ware company.

For the Surly Furious chocolate cake:
Preheat the oven to 375 degrees. In a medium saucepan, bring the beer and butter to a boil. Transfer to a mixing bowl and let cool for at least 10 minutes. Sift the cocoa powder and stir into the beer mixture. Add the sugar and mix well. Beat the eggs and sour cream together and add to the mixing bowl. Sift together the cake flour, baking soda, and salt, add to the batter, and beat until smooth.

Prepare a 12- to 14-cup bundt pan by brushing with shortening or spraying with Baker's Joy. Pour the batter into the pan and bake until a toothpick inserted into the cake comes out clean, 55 to 60 minutes. Allow the cake to cool in the pan, then invert onto a cooling rack.

For the ganache:
Put the chopped chocolate in a medium bowl. In a small saucepan over medium–low heat, simmer the beer until reduced to ¼ cup, about 30 minutes. Add the cream and warm to just below a simmer. Pour the beer and cream over the chocolate and stir continually with a spatula until the chocolate melts and the ganache is smooth.

To assemble:
Pour the ganache over the cooled cake, slice, and serve.

Sweet corn rice pudding

3 cobs sweet corn, shucked

½ cup sweet rice, soaked in cold water overnight

¾ cup sugar

Coconut cream sauce

7 ounces (from a 14-ounce can) Savoy coconut cream

1 ½ teaspoons cornstarch

1 ½ teaspoons sugar

¼ teaspoon salt

½ cup water

Serves 4 to 6

Sweet Corn Rice Pudding

RAINBOW CHINESE RESTAURANT, MINNEAPOLIS
CHEF TAMMY WONG

When sweet corn is in its prime season in Minnesota, we can't get enough of it. This dessert capitalizes on the fresh, sweet flavor of the corn. It's a midwestern twist on a classic Asian dessert made with sticky rice and coconut milk.

For the sweet corn rice pudding:
Cut the kernels of corn off the cob, scraping the kernels down the cob to collect a fair amount of juice from the corn. Drain and rinse the soaked rice, rinsing until the water runs clear. Put the rice and corn together in a medium saucepan with 2 cups of water and bring to a boil over medium heat. Cook until the rice becomes translucent, 10 to 15 minutes. Add the sugar and cook for a couple more minutes. Remove from heat and allow to sit covered for about 30 minutes.

For the coconut cream sauce:
Bring the coconut cream to a simmer in a small saucepan over medium-high heat. In a bowl, whisk the cornstarch, sugar, and salt into ½ cup of water until dissolved. Add this mixture to the simmering coconut cream and stir continuously with a wooden spoon until it comes to a boil and starts to thicken. Remove from heat.

To assemble:
Serve the sweet corn rice pudding in small dishes with the coconut cream sauce poured over top. Enjoy this dessert warm or cold.

Whiskey honey cake

3½ cups flour

1 teaspoon baking powder

1 teaspoon baking soda

½ teaspoon kosher salt

4 teaspoons ground cinnamon

1 teaspoon ground coriander

1 cup canola oil

1 cup (8 ounces) honey

1⅓ cups granulated sugar

½ cup lightly packed brown sugar

3 eggs, lightly beaten

1 teaspoon vanilla extract

1 cup brewed coffee, cold

½ cup hard apple cider

¼ cup whiskey

Whiskey whipped cream filling

2 cups whipping cream

¼ cup powdered sugar

¼ cup whiskey

Garnish

Assorted fresh berries and edible
    flowers such as borage, violas,
    pansies, or nasturtiums

Serves 10 to 12

Whiskey Honey Cake with Whiskey Whipped Cream Filling

ICEHOUSE, MINNEAPOLIS   &   PASTRY CHEF KATIE ELSING

Whiskey, honey, and coffee are great flavor companions, and they play nicely together in this cake. Layer it with whiskey-laced whipped cream filling and garnish with fresh berries and edible flowers from the garden.

For the whiskey honey cake:
Preheat the oven to 300 degrees. (Baking at a low heat keeps the cakes from "doming" so they layer well.) Butter three 8-inch cake rounds and line the bottom of each with parchment paper. Butter the parchment and lightly dust the bottom and sides of each pan with flour.

Sift the flour, baking powder, baking soda, salt, cinnamon, and coriander together into a bowl. In a separate bowl, beat together the canola oil, honey, and granulated and brown sugars, then add the eggs, vanilla, coffee, hard cider, and whiskey. When the batter is smooth, divide equally into the three prepared baking pans and bake until a toothpick inserted into the cakes comes out clean, 40 to 45 minutes.

Allow the cakes to cool for 5 to 10 minutes in the pans, then gently turn them out onto a parchment-lined rack and allow to cool completely before filling.

For the whiskey whipped cream filling:
In a medium bowl, beat the whipped cream until it begins to mound. Slowly beat in the powdered sugar until the mixture forms soft peaks, then stir in the whiskey.

To assemble:
Place one of the cakes on a cake dish or plate. Spoon one-third of the whipped cream onto the cake, then gently layer a second cake tier on top. Spoon another third of the whipped cream onto the second cake, top with the third cake tier, and top with the remaining whipped cream. Garnish with berries and flowers and serve immediately.

(see photograph on page 121)

sources for specialty ingredients

11 Wells Distillery
704 Minnehaha Avenue E
St. Paul, MN 55106
651-300-9328
5oclock@11wells.com
11wells.com

Ames Farm
952-955-3348
webstor.amesfarm@gmail.com
amesfarm.com

Bauhaus Brew Labs
1315 Tyler Street NE
Minneapolis, MN 55413
612-276-6911
info@bauhausbrewlabs.com
bauhausbrewlabs.com

Bent Paddle Brewing Company
1912 West Michigan Street
Duluth, MN 55806
218-279-2722
info@bentpaddlebrewing.com
bentpaddlebrewing.com

Bittercube Bitters
2018 South 1st Street
Milwaukee, WI 53207
414-376-8008
toby@bittercube.com
bittercube.com

Braucher's Sunshine Harvest Farm
2230 35th Street W
Webster, MN 55088
sunshineharvestfarm@hotmail.com
sunshineharvestfarm.com

Broders' Cucina Italiana
2308 West 50th Street
Minneapolis, MN 55410
612-925-3113
broders.com

Caves of Faribault
222 3rd Street NE
Faribault, MN 55021
507-334-5260
info@cavesoffaribault.com
faribaultdairy.com

Dashfire Bitters
76 Western Avenue N
St. Paul, MN 55102
612-229-8593
dashfirebitters@outlook.com
dashfirebitters.com

Du Nord Craft Spirits
2610 East 32nd Street
Minneapolis, MN 55406
612-799-9166
shanelle.montana@dunordcraftspirits.com
dunordcraftspirits.com

Får North Spirits
2045 220th Avenue
Hallock, MN 56728
612-720-3738
info@farnorthspirits.com
farnorthspirits.com

Lone Grazer Creamery
1401 Marshall Street NE
Minneapolis, MN 55413
612-545-5555
info@foodbuilding.com
thelonegrazer.com

Norseman
451 Taft Street NE
Minneapolis, MN 55413
612-643-1933
norsemandistillery.com

Olsen's Fish Company
2115 North 2nd Street
Minneapolis, MN 55411
612-287-0838
lutefisk@olsenfish.com
olsenfish.com

Red Table Meat Company
1401 Marshall Street NE, #100
Minneapolis, MN 55413
612-314-6057
contact@redtablemeatco.com
redtablemeatco.com

Rustica Bakery
3220 West Lake Street
Minneapolis, MN 55416
612-822-1119
rusticabakery.com

Singing Hills Dairy
Nerstrand, MN 55053
507-334-5109
singinghillsgoatdairy@gmail.com

Smude's Sunflower Oil
500 Centennial Drive
Pierz, MN 56364
320-468-6925
smudeoil.com

Stickney Hill Dairy
15371 County Road 48
Kimball, MN 55353
320-398-5360
sales@stickneydairy.com
stickneydairy.com

Surly Brewing Company
520 Malcom Avenue SE
Minneapolis, MN 55414
763-999-4040
beer@surlybrewing.com
surlybrewing.com

Third Street Brewhouse
219 Red River Avenue N
Cold Spring, MN 56320
320-685-3690
thirdstreetbrewhouse.com

Thousand Hills Cattle Company
6492 318th Street
Cannon Falls, MN 55009
877-854-8422
info@thousandhillsgrassfed.com
thousandhillscattleco.com

Vikre Distillery
525 Lake Avenue S, Suite 102
Duluth, MN 55802
218-481-7401
info@vikredistillery.com
vikredistillery.com

Voyageur Brewing Company
233 West Highway 61
Grand Marais, MN 55604
218-387-3163
paul@voyageurbrewing.com
voyageurbrewing.com

contributors

Amboy Cottage Cafe
100 Maine Street E
Amboy, MN 56010
507-674-3123
amboycottagecafe@gmail.com
amboycottagecafe.com

Amy Thielen
Park Rapids, MN
amythielen.com

AZ Canteen
andrewzimmernscanteen.com

The Bachelor Farmer
50 North 2nd Avenue
Minneapolis, MN 55401
612-206-3920
hello@thebachelorfarmer.com
thebachelorfarmer.com

Bonicelli Kitchen
1839 Central Avenue NE
Minneapolis, MN 55418
612-812-3332
laura@bonicellicooks.com
bonicellicooks.com

Breaking Bread Café
1210 West Broadway Avenue
Minneapolis, MN 55411
612-529-9346
info@breakingbreadfoods.com
breakingbreadfoods.com

Broders' Pasta Bar
5000 Penn Avenue S
Minneapolis, MN 55419
612-925-9202
info@broders.com
broders.com

Cafe Levain
4762 Chicago Avenue S
Minneapolis, MN 55407
612-823-7111
vickerman.adam@gmail.com
cafelevain.com

Corner Table
4537 Nicollet Avenue S
Minneapolis, MN 55409
612-823-0011
comments@cornertablerestaurant.com
cornertablerestaurant.com

The Curious Goat
Various locations
Minneapolis, MN
612-229-2364
thecuriousgoateats@gmail.com

The Curry Diva
612-250-6556
curry.diva@gmail.com
thecurrydiva.com

Dashfire Bitters
76 Western Avenue N
St. Paul, MN 55102
612-229-8593
dashfirebitters@outlook.com
dashfirebitters.com

Du Nord Craft Spirits
2610 East 32nd Street
Minneapolis, MN 55406
612-382-7236
shanelle.montana@dunordcraftspirits.com
dunordcraftspirits.com

The Elephant Walk B & B
801 West Pine Street
Stillwater, MN 55082
651-430-0359
rita@elephantwalkbb.com
elephantwalkbb.com

Får North Spirits
2045 220th Avenue
Hallock, MN 56728
612-720-3738
info@farnorthspirits.com
farnorthspirits.com

Food Works
5009 Excelsior Boulevard, #108
St. Louis Park, MN 55416
952-926-8442
info@andrewzimmern.com
andrewzimmern.com

Forepaugh's
276 Exchange Street
St. Paul, MN 55102
651-224-5606
chef@forepaughs.com
forepaughs.com

Gai Gai Thai
Various locations
Minneapolis, MN
612-991-9923
eat@gaigaithai.com

Good Life Catering
See their Facebook page

Green Scene
617 Michigan Avenue W
Walker, MN 56484
218-547-2880
erin@walkergreenscene.com
walkergreenscene.com

GYST Fermentation Bar
25 East 26th Street
Minneapolis, MN 55404
612-758-0113
info@gystmpls.com
gystmpls.com

Heartland Restaurant
289 East 5th Street
St. Paul, MN 55101
651-699-3536
heartland5@qwestoffice.net
heartlandrestaurant.com

Hell's Kitchen
80 South 9th Street
Minneapolis, MN 55402
612-332-4700
hellskitchen@visi.com
hellskitcheninc.com

Heyday
2700 Lyndale Avenue S
Minneapolis, MN 55408
612-200-9369
heydayeats.com

Hola Arepa
3501 Nicollet Avenue S
Minneapolis, MN 55408
612-345-5583
eat@holaarepa.com
holaarepa.com

Honey and Rye Bakehouse
4501 Excelsior Boulevard
St. Louis Park, MN 55416
612-844-2555
info@honey-and-rye.com
honey-and-rye.com

Icehouse
2528 Nicollet Avenue S
Minneapolis, MN 55404
612-276-6523
matt@icehousempls.com
icehousempls.com

Insula Restaurant
145 East Sheridan Street
Ely, MN 55731
218-365-4855
daniel@insularestaurant.com
insularestaurant.com

Jenny Breen
Minneapolis, MN
jennybroccoli@yahoo.com
goodlifecooking.net

The Kenwood
2115 West 21st Street
Minneapolis, MN 55405
612-377-3695
don@thekenwoodrestaurant.com
thekenwoodrestaurant.com

Kitchen in the Market
920 East Lake Street
Minneapolis, MN 55407
612-470-1056
molly@kitcheninthemarket.com
kitcheninthemarket.com

La Ferme
613 Broadway Street
Alexandria, MN 56308
320-846-0777
broadwaybistroalex@gmail.com
broadwaybistroalex.com

Lake Avenue Restaurant
394 South Lake Avenue
Duluth, MN 55802
218-722-2355
lakeavenuecafe@gmail.com
lakeavenuerestaurantandbar.com

Lola—An American Bistro
16 North Minnesota Street
New Ulm, MN 56073
507-359-2500
llueth@yahoo.com
lolaamericanbistro.com

Lucia's
1432 West 31st Street
Minneapolis, MN 55408
612-825-1572
ryan@lucias.com
lucias.com

Maplelag Resort
30501 Maplelag Road
Callaway, MN 56521
218-375-2267
jrichard@arvig.net
maplelag.com

New Scenic Café
5461 North Shore Drive
Duluth, MN 55804
218-525-6274
scott@newsceniccafe
newsceniccafe.com

Nosh
310-1/2 South Washington St.
Lake City, MN 55041
651-345-2425
mail@noshrestaurant.com
noshrestaurant.com

Patisserie 46
4552 Grand Avenue S
Minneapolis, MN 55419
612-208-1583
catering@patisserie46.com
patisserie46.com

Prairie Bay Grill & Catering
15115 Edgewood Drive
Baxter, MN 56425
218-330-5881
matt@yahoo.com
prairiebay.com

A Proper Pour
Minneapolis, MN
571-262-1762
info@aproperpour.com

The Rabbit Hole
920 East Lake Street
Minneapolis, MN 55407
612-236-4526
info@eatdrinkrabbit.com
eatdrinkrabbit.com

Rainbow Chinese Restaurant
2739 Nicollet Avenue S
Minneapolis, MN 55408
612-870-7084
tammy@rainbowrestaurant.com
rainbowrestaurant.com

Robin Asbell
robin@robinasbell.com
robinasbell.com

The Salt Cellar
173 Western Avenue
St. Paul, MN 55102
651-219-4013
alanbergo3@gmail.com
saltcellarsaintpaul.com

Salty Tart
920 East Lake Street
Minneapolis, MN 55407
952-681-8195
chefgayer@gmail.com
saltytart.com

Scandinavian Inn
701 Kenilworth Ave S
Lanesboro, MN 55949
507-467-4500
scandinavianinn@acegroup.com
scandinavianinn.com

Sen Yai Sen Lek
2422 Central Avenue NE
Minneapolis, MN 55418
612-781-3046
joe@senyai-senlek.com
senyai-senlek.com

Spoon and Stable
211 1st Street N
Minneapolis, MN 55401
612-224-9850
gavin@spoonandstable.com
spoonandstable.com

Spoonriver
750 South 2nd Street
Minneapolis, MN 55401
612-436-2236
brenda@spoonriver.com
spoonriver.com

Terzo
2221 West 50th Street
Minneapolis, MN 55419
612-925-0330
thomas@broders.com
terzompls.com

That Food Girl
thatfoodgirl.com

The Third Bird
1612 Harmon Place
Minneapolis, MN 55403
612-767-9495
lucas@thethirdbirdmpls.com
thethirdbirdmpls.com

The Three Crows
225 North River Street
Delano, MN 55328
763-972-3399
gina@thethreecrows.com
thethreecrows.com

Tongue in Cheek
989 Payne Avenue
St. Paul, MN 55130
651-888-6148
chef@tongueincheek.biz
tongueincheek.biz

True Cost Farm
4432 County Road 12
Montrose, MN 55363
612-217-1770
info@tc.farm
tc.farm

Victory 44
2203 North 44th Avenue
Minneapolis, MN 55412
612-588-2228
victory-44.com

Vikre Distillery
525 Lake Avenue S
Duluth, MN 55802
218-481-7401
emily@vikredistillery.com
vikredistillery.com

Voyageur Brewing Company
233 West Highway 61
Grand Marais, MN 55604
218-387-3163
info@voyageurbrewing.com
voyageurbrewing.com

Waves of Superior Cafe
20 Surfside Drive
Tofte, MN 55615
218-663-6877
judi@bluefinbay.com
surfsideonsuperior.com

The Wedge & Wheel
308 Chestnut Street E
Stillwater, MN 55082
651-342-1687
info@wedgeandwheel.com
wedgeandwheel.com

Wild Hare Bistro
523 Minnesota Ave NW
Bemidji, MN 56601
218-444-5282
wildhare@paulbunyan.net
wildharebistro.com

Wise Acre Eatery
5401 Nicollet Avenue S
Minneapolis, MN 55419
612-354-2577
info@wiseacreeatery.com
wiseacreeatery.com

Zzest Café & Bar
1190 16th Street SW, #600
Rochester, MN 55902
507-424-0080
LeeAnn@zzestmarket.com
zzest.com

Zoë François (Zoë Bakes)
Minneapolis, MN
zoebakes.com

index

A

açai
    Raw Vegetable Salad with Açai Vinaigrette, 52
aioli, 96–97
Almendinger, Lucas, 2
Almond French Toast with Roasted Strawberry Jam
    and Brown Sugar Cream, 2
almonds
    Almond French Toast with Roasted Strawberry Jam
        and Brown Sugar Cream, 2
    Plum Frangipane Tart, 140–141
    Wild Rice Salad with Maple-Toasted Almonds, 62
Amboy Cottage Cafe, 112–113, 148
Anderson, Leonard, 25, 137–138
Andrus, Anne, 59, 132
Annand, Matt, 34–35
Apple and Smoked Gouda Turnovers, 22
Apple-Ginger Bread Pudding, 122
apples
    Apple and Smoked Gouda Turnovers, 22
    Apple-Ginger Bread Pudding, 122
arugula
    Lutefisk Benedict, 12–13
    Roasted Beet Salad with Sherry Pepper Vinaigrette, 53
Asbell, Robin, 56–57, 73, 149
asparagus
    Lamb Chops with Spring Vegetables, 100
    Minnesota "Nice-oise" Salad with Salmon, 51
    Wild Rice Orzotto with Morels, Ramps, and Hazelnuts, 61
AZ Canteen, 119

B

Bachelor Farmer, The, 36–37, 38, 148
bacon
    Bacon-Glazed Brussels Sprouts, 42
    Beer and Bacon Caramel Sundae, 123
    Fried Green Tomatoes with Skillet Sweet Corn
        Vinaigrette, 29–31
    Lutefisk Benedict, 12–13
    Okonomiyaki, 15
Bacon-Glazed Brussels Sprouts, 42
barbecue sauce, rhubarb, 98
Barsness, Judi, 61
Bauer, Ann, 9–11
beans
    Squash and Wild Rice Chili, 73
    Tofu Veggie Breakfast Tacos, 18
    Wild Hare Cuban Breakfast Burritos, 19
beans, garbanzo
    Beet Hummus, 24
beans, green
    Grilled Bean Slaw, 48–49
    Seared Duck Breast and Amarena Cherries, 114–115
    Tod Mun Pla: Curried Fish Cakes with Cucumber Salad, 39
Beebopareebop Strawberry Rhubarb Cocktail, 78

beef
    Beef Wellington with Swiss Chard and
        Mushroom Duxelles, 86
    Braised Beef Pot Roast, 88
    Surly Bender Braised Short Ribs, 117
    Sweet Crispy Beef with Coriander Seed
        (Nuea Dat Deow), 118
beef, ground
    Maple Stout Sloppy Joes, 105
Beef Wellington with Swiss Chard and
    Mushroom Duxelles, 86
beer
    Beer and Bacon Caramel Sundae, 123
    Beer-Battered Squash Blossoms Stuffed
        with Cheese Curds, 23
    Maple Stout Sloppy Joes, 105
    Molten Chocolate Cakes with Beer Ice Cream, 139
    Surly Bender Braised Short Ribs, 117
    Surly Furious Chocolate Bundt Cake, 144
    Voyageur Brewing Beer Cheese Fondue, 40
Beer and Bacon Caramel Sundae, 123
Beer-Battered Squash Blossoms Stuffed with Cheese Curds, 23
Beet Hummus, 24
beets
    Beet Hummus, 24
    Raw Vegetable Salad with Açai Vinaigrette, 52
    Roasted Beet Salad with Sherry Pepper Vinaigrette, 53
Beran, Tony, 12–13, 41, 44–45, 63, 70, 106–107
Berglund, Paul, 36–37, 38
Bergo, Alan, 43, 94–95, 96–97
berries
    Lemon Riccota Hotcakes, 9–11
    Raw Vegetable Salad with Açai Vinaigrette, 52
    Whiskey Honey Cake with Whiskey Whipped Cream
        Filling, 121, 146
Bickford, Matt, 42, 47
bison
    Bison Burger, 85, 87
Bizarre Foods, 119
blueberries
    Blueberry Bars with Lemon-Thyme Shortbread Crust, 124–125
    Honey-Vanilla Cheesecake with Blueberry Caramel Sauce,
        134–136
Blueberry Bars with Lemon-Thyme Shortbread Crust, 124–125
Boemer, Thomas, 26–27
Bonicelli, Laura, 68–69, 142
Bonicelli Kitchen, 68–69, 142, 148
bourbon
    Dashfire Bitters "New Fashioned," 77, 79
Braised Beef Pot Roast, 88
Braised Duck Legs with Creamy Farro and Orange, 89–91
Braised Pork Belly, 25
Braised Pork Shank Ossobuco with Herb Gremolata
    (Ossobuco di Maiale), 92–93

bread
    Almond French Toast with Roasted Strawberry Jam
        and Brown Sugar Cream, 2
    Apple-Ginger Bread Pudding, 122
    Bison Burger, 85, 87
    Maple Stout Sloppy Joes, 105
    Pepito Ancho Butter and Pumpkin Jam Sandwiches, 106–107
    Prairie Bay's BYOB (Build Your Own Bruschetta), 34–35
    Smoked Trout, Scrambled Eggs, Capers, and Trout Roe
        on Buttered Toast, 36–37
    Tomato-Fennel Soup with "Inside Out" Grilled
        Cheese Sandwiches, 74–75
bread, sourdough
    Savory Bread Pudding, 59
bread pudding
    Apple-Ginger Bread Pudding, 122
    Savory Bread Pudding, 59
Breaking Bread Café, 4–5, 18, 148
Breen, Jenny, 51, 149
Brined Turkey with Pan Jus and Caramelized Salsify, 94–95
Broccoli and Sun-dried Tomato Quiche, 3
Broder, Thomas, 64, 92–93, 104
Broders' Pasta Bar, 148
Broders' Restaurant, 104
Brussels sprouts
Bacon-Glazed Brussels Sprouts, 42
Burdock Mashed Potatoes, 43
burritos
    Wild Hare Cuban Breakfast Burritos, 19
butter, pepito ancho, 106–107
Buttered Popcorn Gnocchi with Port Wine Reduction, 41, 44–45
Buttered Popcorn Pot de Crème, 126–127
buttermilk
    Buttermilk Herb Biscuits and Chorizo-Poblano Gravy, 4–5
    Green Goddess Dressing, 47
    Pork Loin Katsu with Sesame Basil Pesto and Fingerling
        Potato Confit, 108–109
Buttermilk Herb Biscuits and Chorizo-Poblano Gravy, 4–5

C
cabbage
    Grilled Bean Slaw, 48–49
    Okonomiyaki, 15
Cafe Levain, 58, 88, 148
cake
    Surly Furious Chocolate Bundt Cake, 144
    Whiskey Honey Cake with Whiskey Whipped Cream
        Filling, 121, 146
capers
    Linguine Bianco e Nero, 104
    Minnesota "Nice-oise" Salad with Salmon, 51
    Smoked Trout, Scrambled Eggs, Capers, and Trout Roe
        on Buttered Toast, 36–37
caramel
    Beer and Bacon Caramel Sundae, 123
    Honey-Vanilla Cheesecake with Blueberry Caramel Sauce,
        134–136
Carrot-Family Slaw with Dill and Cilantro, 46
carrots
    Carrot-Family Slaw with Dill and Cilantro, 46
    Gai Gai Thai Breakfast Bowl, 7–8

Raw Vegetable Salad with Açai Vinaigrette, 52
    Roasted Root Vegetables, 58
cauliflower
    Roasted Cauliflower with Mint, Golden Raisins, Cornichons,
        and Parmesan, 54–55
Chanterelles à la Greque, 26–27
Charred Bell Pepper Soup with Chèvre and Balsamic Vinegar, 64
Charred Red Lentil Dhal, 65
Cheddar Grits with Ham, Kale, and Fried Duck Egg, 6
cheese
    Apple and Smoked Gouda Turnovers, 22
    Beer-Battered Squash Blossoms Stuffed with Cheese Curds, 23
    Braised Duck Legs with Creamy Farro and Orange, 89–91
    Broccoli and Sun-dried Tomato Quiche, 3
    Buttered Popcorn Gnocchi with Port Wine Reduction, 41, 44–45
    Charred Bell Pepper Soup with Chèvre and Balsamic Vinegar, 64
    Cheddar Grits with Ham, Kale, and Fried Duck Egg, 6
    Goat Cheese, Honey, Date, and Pistachio Truffles, 133
    Lemon Riccota Hotcakes, 9–11
    Linguine Bianco e Nero, 104
    Pork Loin Katsu with Sesame Basil Pesto and Fingerling
        Potato Confit, 108–109
    Prairie Bay's BYOB (Build Your Own Bruschetta), 34–35
    Roasted Cauliflower with Mint, Golden Raisins, Cornichons,
        and Parmesan, 54–55
    Roasted Ramps and Watercress with Pumpkin Seed Chèvre
        Medallions, 56–57
    Salmon and Cheddar Quiche, 112–113
    Savory Bread Pudding, 59
    Tomato-Fennel Soup with "Inside Out" Grilled Cheese
        Sandwiches, 74–75
    Voyageur Brewing Beer Cheese Fondue, 40
    Wild Hare Cuban Breakfast Burritos, 19
    Wild Hare Smoky Squash Chowder, 76
    Wild Rice Orzotto with Morels, Ramps, and Hazelnuts, 61
    See also chèvre
cheesecake
    Honey-Vanilla Cheesecake with Blueberry Caramel Sauce,
        134–136
    Mascarpone No-Bake Cheesecake with Chocolate-Graham
        Soil, 137–138
cherries
    Cherry Pecan Scones, 128
    Seared Duck Breast and Amarena Cherries, 114–115
Cherry Pecan Scones, 128
Chestnut Crème Brûlée with Cognac-Marinated Prunes, 129
chicken
    Gai Gai Thai Breakfast Bowl, 7–8
    Grilled Chicken with Rhubarb Barbecue Sauce, 98
    Roasted Chicken Thighs with Clams, Rapini, and Dill
        Mayonnaise, 110–111
chicken broth, stock
    Braised Duck Legs with Creamy Farro and Orange, 89–91
    Braised Pork Shank Ossobuco with Herb Gremolata
        (Ossobuco di Maiale), 92–93
    Brined Turkey with Pan Jus and Caramelized Salsify, 94–95
    Okonomiyaki, 15
    Wild Hare Smoky Squash Chowder, 76
    Wild Rice Orzotto with Morels, Ramps, and Hazelnuts, 61
chile peppers. *See* peppers, chile

chili
    Squash and Wild Rice Chili, 73
    Wild Hare Cuban Breakfast Burritos, 19
chocolate
    Mascarpone No-Bake Cheesecake with Chocolate-Graham
        Soil, 137–138
    Molten Chocolate Cakes with Beer Ice Cream, 139
    Surly Furious Chocolate Bundt Cake, 144
chorizo
    Buttermilk Herb Biscuits and Chorizo-Poblano Gravy, 4–5
chowder
    Grilled Corn and Potato Chowder, 68–69
    Lake Superior Trout and Pumpkin Chowder, 63, 70
    Wild Hare Smoky Squash Chowder, 76
Christiansen, Jim, 110–111
clams
    Roasted Chicken Thighs with Clams, Rapini, and
        Dill Mayonnaise, 110–111
Coburn, Gina, 17
coconut cream, milk
    Charred Red Lentil Dhal, 65
    Gai Gai Thai Breakfast Bowl, 7–8
    Pepita Granola, 16
    Sweet Corn Rice Pudding, 145
coffee
    Whiskey Honey Cake with Whiskey Whipped Cream
        Filling, 121, 146
Conroy, Charles, 40, 125
cookies
    Ginger Ginger Cookies, 132
corn
    Fried Green Tomatoes with Skillet Sweet Corn
        Vinaigrette, 29–31
    Grilled Corn and Potato Chowder, 68–69
    Grilled Minnesota Pork Loin with Sweet Corn Relish, 99
    Sommer Pasta, 116
    Sweet Corn Rice Pudding, 145
Corner Table, 26–27, 148
cornmeal
    Cornmeal Sunfish with Pickled Ramp Aioli, 96–97
    Fried Green Tomatoes with Skillet Sweet Corn
        Vinaigrette, 29–31
Cornmeal Sunfish with Pickled Ramp Aioli, 96–97
cranberries
    Cranberry-Orange Bread, 130–131
cranberry juice
    Steady Eddie, 84
Cranberry-Orange Bread, 130–131
cream
    Almond French Toast with Roasted Strawberry Jam
        and Brown Sugar Cream, 2
    Apple-Ginger Bread Pudding, 122
    Beer and Bacon Caramel Sundae, 123
    Braised Duck Legs with Creamy Farro and Orange, 89–91
    Burdock Mashed Potatoes, 43
    Buttered Popcorn Pot de Crème, 126–127
    Buttermilk Herb Biscuits and Chorizo-Poblano Gravy, 4–5
    Cherry Pecan Scones, 128
    Chestnut Crème Brûlée with Cognac-Marinated Prunes, 129
    Grilled Corn and Potato Chowder, 68–69
    Lake Superior Trout and Pumpkin Chowder, 63, 70

    Lamb Meatballs with Soft Polenta, Red Pepper Jus,
        and Parsley-Red Onion Salad, 101–103
    Linguine Bianco e Nero, 104
    Mascarpone No-Bake Cheesecake with Chocolate-Graham
        Soil, 137–138
    Molten Chocolate Cakes with Beer Ice
        Cream, 139
    Roasted Garlic and Nettle Soup, 71
    Savory Bread Pudding, 59
    Sommer Pasta, 116
    Surly Furious Chocolate Bundt Cake, 144
    Voyageur Brewing Beer Cheese Fondue, 40
cream cheese
    Blueberry Bars with Lemon-Thyme
        Shortbread Crust, 124–125
    Honey-Vanilla Cheesecake with Blueberry
        Caramel Sauce, 134–136
    Mascarpone No-Bake Cheesecake with
        Chocolate-Graham Soil, 137–138
crème brûlée
    Chestnut Crème Brûlée with Cognac-Marinated Prunes, 129
cucumbers
    Får North Spirits Cucumber Cosmopolitan, 80
    Green Gazpacho with Chive Sour Cream, 66–67
    Lola Refrigerator Pickles, 21, 33
    Tod Mun Pla: Curried Fish Cakes with Cucumber Salad, 39
Cunningham, Lachelle, 4–5, 18
Curious Goat, The, 53, 100, 148
curry
    Charred Red Lentil Dhal, 65
    Gai Gai Thai Breakfast Bowl, 7–8
    Tod Mun Pla: Curried Fish Cakes with Cucumber Salad, 39
Curry Diva, The, 65, 148

D
Dashfire Bitters, 79, 148
Dashfire Bitters "New Fashioned," 77, 79
dates
    Goat Cheese, Honey, Date, and Pistachio Truffles, 133
dill
    Carrot-Family Slaw with Dill and Cilantro, 46
    Roasted Chicken Thighs with Clams, Rapini, and Dill
        Mayonnaise, 110–111
dressings, 48, 51
    Green Goddess Dressing, 47
duck
    Braised Duck Legs with Creamy Farro and Orange, 89–91
    Seared Duck Breast and Amarena Cherries, 114–115
Du Nord Craft Spirits, 84, 148

E
eggs
    Almond French Toast with Roasted Strawberry Jam
        and Brown Sugar Cream, 2
    Apple-Ginger Bread Pudding, 122
    Broccoli and Sun-dried Tomato Quiche, 3
    Buttered Popcorn Pot de Crème, 126–127
    Cheddar Grits with Ham, Kale, and Fried Duck Egg, 6
    Chestnut Crème Brûlée with Cognac-Marinated Prunes, 129
    Fried Green Tomatoes with Skillet Sweet Corn
        Vinaigrette, 29–31

Gai Gai Thai Breakfast Bowl, 7–8
Honey-Vanilla Cheesecake with Blueberry Caramel Sauce,
    134–136
Lemon Riccota Hotcakes, 9–11
Lutefisk Benedict, 12–13
Minnesota "Nice-oise" Salad with Salmon, 51
Molten Chocolate Cakes with Beer Ice Cream, 139
Norwegian Pancakes, 1, 14
Okonomiyaki, 15
Salmon and Cheddar Quiche, 112–113
Smoked Trout, Scrambled Eggs, Capers, and Trout Roe
    on Buttered Toast, 36–37
Wild Hare Cuban Breakfast Burritos, 19
Elephant Walk Bed and Breakfast, 15, 148
Elsing, Katie, 121, 146

F
Fàr North Spirits, 80, 81, 148
Fàr North Spirits Cucumber Cosmopolitan, 80
Fàr North Spirits Oak Island Rum Punch, 81
farro
    Braised Duck Legs with Creamy Farro and Orange, 89–91
Fermented Herb Yogurt Dip, 28
figs
    Seared Duck Breast and Amarena Cherries, 114–115
fish
    Cornmeal Sunfish with Pickled Ramp Aioli, 96–97
    Lake Superior Trout and Pumpkin Chowder, 63, 70
    Lutefisk Benedict, 12–13
    Minnesota "Nice-oise" Salad with Salmon, 51
    Salmon and Cheddar Quiche, 112–113
    Smoked Trout, Scrambled Eggs, Capers, and Trout Roe on
        Buttered Toast, 36–37
    Soused Herring, 38
    Tod Mun Pla: Curried Fish Cakes with Cucumber Salad, 39
    Walleye with Sesame Crust and Ginger-Orange Teriyaki, 120
Fisher, Beth, 24, 29–31
Food Works, 119, 148
Forepaugh's, 86, 148
François, Zoë, 124–125, 150
French toast
    Almond French Toast with Roasted Strawberry Jam
        and Brown Sugar Cream, 2
Fried Green Tomatoes with Skillet Sweet Corn Vinaigrette, 29–31

G
Gai Gai Thai, 7–8, 148
Gai Gai Thai Breakfast Bowl, 7–8
garlic
    Bacon-Glazed Brussels Sprouts, 42
    Braised Beef Pot Roast, 88
    Brined Turkey with Pan Jus and Caramelized Salsify, 94–95
    Prairie Bay's BYOB (Build Your Own Bruschetta), 34–35
    Roasted Garlic and Nettle Soup, 71
    Sofrito Potatoes, 60
Gayer, Michelle, 144
gazpacho
    Green Gazpacho with Chive Sour Cream, 66–67
gin
    Beebopareebop Strawberry Rhubarb Cocktail, 78
    Fàr North Spirits Cucumber Cosmopolitan, 80

Norseman Strawberry Rhubarb Fizz, 82
Nothing Gold Can Stay, 83
Steady Eddie, 84
ginger
    Apple-Ginger Bread Pudding, 122
    Ginger Ginger Cookies, 132
Ginger Ginger Cookies, 132
gnocchi
    Buttered Popcorn Gnocchi with Port Wine Reduction, 41, 44–45
Goat Cheese, Honey, Date, and Pistachio Truffles, 133
Gonzales, Donald, 86
Good Life Catering, 51
"Gotta Have It" Chicken Liver Pâté, 32
Graden, Scott, 52, 114–115
graham crackers
    Honey-Vanilla Cheesecake with Blueberry Caramel Sauce,
        134–136
    Mascarpone No-Bake Cheesecake with Chocolate-Graham
        Soil, 137–138
granola
    Pepita Granola, 16
gravy
    Buttermilk Herb Biscuits and Chorizo-Poblano Gravy, 4–5
Gray, Ian, 53, 100
Graybill, Rita, 15
Green Gazpacho with Chive Sour Cream, 66–67
Green Goddess Dressing, 47
Green Scene, 62, 105, 148
gremolata, herb, 92–93
Grilled Bean Slaw, 48–49
Grilled Chicken with Rhubarb Barbecue Sauce, 98
Grilled Corn and Potato Chowder, 68–69
Grilled Minnesota Pork Loin with Sweet Corn Relish, 99
grits
    Cheddar Grits with Ham, Kale, and Fried Duck Egg, 6
Guse, Melanie, 28
GYST Fermentation Bar, 28, 148

H
Haefele, Erin, 62, 105
ham
    Cheddar Grits with Ham, Kale, and Fried Duck Egg, 6
Harcey, Erick, 74–75, 126–127
Hatch-Surisook, Joe, 39, 118
Heartland Restaurant, 66–67, 99, 148
Hell's Kitchen, 9–11, 85, 87, 148
herring
    Soused Herring, 38
Herrmann, Molly, 22, 143
Heyday, 110–111, 149
Hola Arepa, 16, 60, 149
Honey and Rye Bakehouse, 59, 132, 149
Honey-Vanilla Cheesecake with Blueberry Caramel Sauce,
    134–136

I
ice cream
    Beer and Bacon Caramel Sundae, 123
    Molten Chocolate Cakes with Beer Ice Cream, 139
Icehouse, 42, 47, 121, 146, 149
Insula Restaurant, 117, 134–136, 149

J

jam
    pumpkin, 106–107
    roasted strawberry, 2
    Rosemary Rhubarb Jam, 143
    sun-dried tomato, 34–35
Jansz, Heather, 65
Jaworski, Greg, 71
Jensen, Matthew, 116, 139
jus, 94–95, 101–103

K

kale
    Cheddar Grits with Ham, Kale, and Fried Duck Egg, 6
    Savory Bread Pudding, 59
Kaysen, Gavin, 89–91
Kenwood Restaurant, The, 6, 129, 149
Kim, Heather, 16
Kim, Thomas, 108–109
Kitchen in the Market, 22, 143, 149
Kohtz, Chris, 133
Kraus, John, 128, 140–141

L

La Ferme, 116, 139, 149
Lake Avenue Restaurant, 12–13, 41, 44–45, 63, 70, 106–107, 149
Lake Superior Trout and Pumpkin Chowder, 63, 70
Lamb Chops with Spring Vegetables, 100
Lamb Meatballs with Soft Polenta, Red Pepper Jus, and
    Parsley-Red Onion Salad, 101–103
Langton, Brenda, 120, 130–131
Lemongrass Pork Tenderloin over Mixed Greens, 50
Lemon Riccota Hotcakes, 9–11
lentils
    Charred Red Lentil Dhal, 65
lettuce
    Roasted Ramps and Watercress with Pumpkin Seed Chèvre
    Medallions, 56–57
Lindberg, Lisa, 112–113
Linguine Bianco e Nero, 104
liver, chicken
    "Gotta Have It" Chicken Liver Pâté, 32
Lola-An American Bistro, 20, 21, 33, 149
Lola Refrigerator Pickles, 21, 33
Lucia's Restaurant, 48–49, 72, 149
Lueth, Lacey, 20, 21, 33
Lund, Ryan, 48–49, 72
Lutefisk Benedict, 12–13

M

Maplelag Resort, 1, 14, 149
Maple Stout Sloppy Joes, 105
maple syrup
    Nothing Gold Can Stay, 83
Mascarpone No-Bake Cheesecake with Chocolate-Graham
    Soil, 137–138
mayonnaise
    Okonomiyaki, 15
mayonnaise, dill, 110–111
McCann, Betsy, 32
McCann, Jack, 32

melon
    Green Gazpacho with Chive Sour Cream, 66–67
milk
    Apple-Ginger Bread Pudding, 122
    Buttered Popcorn Pot de Crème, 126–127
Minnesota "Nice-oise" Salad with Salmon, 51
miso
    Venison Tenderloin with Miso Sauce, 119
Molten Chocolate Cakes with Beer Ice Cream, 139
Montana, Chris, 84
mushrooms
    Beef Wellington with Swiss Chard and Mushroom Duxelles, 86
    Broccoli and Sun-dried Tomato Quiche, 3
    Chanterelles à la Greque, 26–27
    "Gotta Have It" Chicken Liver Pâté, 32
    Prairie Bay's BYOB (Build Your Own Bruschetta), 34–35
    Wild Rice Orzotto with Morels, Ramps, and Hazelnuts, 61

N

Nelson, Betsy, 23, 98
nettles
    Roasted Garlic and Nettle Soup, 71
New Midwestern Table, The, 46, 122
New Scenic Café, 52, 114–115, 149
Nguyen, Christina, 60
Norseman Strawberry Rhubarb Fizz, 82
Norwegian Pancakes, 1, 14
Nosh Restaurant and Bar, 71, 149
Nothing Gold Can Stay, 83
nuts. *See* almonds, hazelnuts, pecans, pistachios

O

Okonomiyaki, 15
olives
    Linguine Bianco e Nero, 104
Olk, Deb, 1, 14
Omer, Mitch, 9–11, 85, 87
onions
    Braised Beef Pot Roast, 88
    Braised Pork Shank Ossobuco with Herb Gremolata
    (Ossobuco di Maiale), 92–93
    Charred Bell Pepper Soup with Chèvre and Balsamic Vinegar, 64
    Charred Red Lentil Dhal, 65
    Fried Green Tomatoes with Skillet Sweet Corn Vinaigrette, 29–31
    "Gotta Have It" Chicken Liver Pâté, 32
    Green Gazpacho with Chive Sour Cream, 66–67
    Grilled Minnesota Pork Loin with Sweet Corn Relish, 99
    Lamb Chops with Spring Vegetables, 100
    Lamb Meatballs with Soft Polenta, Red Pepper Jus, and
    Parsley-Red Onion Salad, 101–103
    Maple Stout Sloppy Joes, 105
    Soused Herring, 38
oranges
    Braised Duck Legs with Creamy Farro and Orange, 89–91
    Cranberry-Orange Bread, 130–131
    Mascarpone No-Bake Cheesecake with Chocolate-Graham
    Soil, 137–138

P

pancakes
    Lemon Riccota Hotcakes, 9–11

Norwegian Pancakes, 1, 14
Okonomiyaki, 15
Three Crows Minnesota Flappers, 17
parsnips
    Roasted Root Vegetables, 58
pasta
    Linguine Bianco e Nero, 104
    Sommer Pasta, 116
pastry
    Apple and Smoked Gouda Turnovers, 22
    Beef Wellington with Swiss Chard and Mushroom Duxelles, 86
    Broccoli and Sun-dried Tomato Quiche, 3
    Plum Frangipane Tart, 140–141
    Raspberry Galette, 142
    Salmon and Cheddar Quiche, 112–113
pâté
    "Gotta Have It" Chicken Liver Pâté, 32
Patisserie 46, 128, 140–141, 149
pecans
    Cherry Pecan Scones, 128
Pepita Granola, 16
pepitas. *See* pumpkin seeds
Pepito Ancho Butter and Pumpkin Jam Sandwiches, 106–107
peppers, bell
    Charred Bell Pepper Soup with Chèvre and Balsamic Vinegar, 64
    Green Gazpacho with Chive Sour Cream, 66–67
    Lamb Meatballs with Soft Polenta, Red Pepper Jus, and
        Parsley-Red Onion Salad, 101–103
    Maple Stout Sloppy Joes, 105
    Prairie Bay's BYOB (Build Your Own Bruschetta), 34–35
    Sofrito Potatoes, 60
    Tofu Veggie Breakfast Tacos, 18
peppers, chile
    Buttermilk Herb Biscuits and Chorizo-Poblano Gravy, 4–5
    Fermented Herb Yogurt Dip, 28
    Gai Gai Thai Breakfast Bowl, 7–8
    Green Gazpacho with Chive Sour Cream, 66–67
    Grilled Chicken with Rhubarb Barbecue Sauce, 98
    Pepito Ancho Butter and Pumpkin Jam Sandwiches, 106–107
    Sweet Crispy Beef with Coriander Seed (Nuea Dat Deow), 118
pestos, 34–35, 108–109
Petcharawises, Kris, 7–8
pickles
    Lola Refrigerator Pickles, 21, 33
pistachios
    Goat Cheese, Honey, Date, and Pistachio Truffles, 133
Plum Frangipane Tart, 140–141
polenta
    Lamb Meatballs with Soft Polenta, Red Pepper Jus, and
        Parsley-Red Onion Salad, 101–103
popcorn
    Buttered Popcorn Gnocchi with Port Wine Reduction, 41, 44–45
    Buttered Popcorn Pot de Crème, 126–127
pork
    Braised Pork Belly, 25
    Braised Pork Shank Ossobuco with Herb Gremolata
        (Ossobuco di Maiale), 92–93
    Grilled Minnesota Pork Loin with Sweet Corn Relish, 99
    Lemongrass Pork Tenderloin over Mixed Greens, 50
    Pork Loin Katsu with Sesame Basil Pesto and Fingerling
        Potato Confit, 108–109

pork, ground
    Lamb Meatballs with Soft Polenta, Red Pepper Jus, and
        Parsley-Red Onion Salad, 101–103
    Pork Loin Katsu with Sesame Basil Pesto and Fingerling
        Potato Confit, 108–109
potatoes
    Burdock Mashed Potatoes, 43
    Grilled Corn and Potato Chowder, 68–69
    Minnesota "Nice-oise" Salad with Salmon, 51
    Pork Loin Katsu with Sesame Basil Pesto and Fingerling
        Potato Confit, 108–109
    Sofrito Potatoes, 60
    Wild Hare Smoky Squash Chowder, 76
Prairie Bay Grill, 34–35, 149
Prairie Bay's BYOB (Build Your Own Bruschetta), 34–35
Proper Pour, A, 82, 149
prunes
    Chestnut Crème Brûlée with Cognac-Marinated Prunes, 129
pumpkin
    Lake Superior Trout and Pumpkin Chowder, 63, 70
    Pepito Ancho Butter and Pumpkin Jam Sandwiches, 106–107
pumpkin seeds
    Pepita Granola, 16
    Pepito Ancho Butter and Pumpkin Jam Sandwiches, 106–107
    Roasted Ramps and Watercress with Pumpkin Seed Chèvre
        Medallions, 56–57
    Roasted Squash and Sweet Potato Soup with Hazelnut Oil
        and Saba, 72

Q
quiche
    Broccoli and Sun-dried Tomato Quiche, 3
    Salmon and Cheddar Quiche, 112–113
quinoa
    Wild Rice and Quinoa Porridge, 20

R
Rabbit Hole, The, 108–109, 149
radishes
    Raw Vegetable Salad with Açaí Vinaigrette, 52
Rainbow Chinese Restaurant, 50, 145, 149
raisins
    Roasted Cauliflower with Mint, Golden Raisins,
        Cornichons, and Parmesan, 54–55
ramps
    Cornmeal Sunfish with Pickled Ramp Aioli, 96–97
    Roasted Ramps and Watercress with Pumpkin Seed
        Chèvre Medallions, 56–57
    Wild Rice Orzotto with Morels, Ramps, and Hazelnuts, 61
rapini
    Roasted Chicken Thighs with Clams, Rapini, and Dill
        Mayonnaise, 110–111
raspberries
    Raspberry Galette, 142
    Roasted Ramps and Watercress with Pumpkin Seed
        Chèvre Medallions, 56–57
Raspberry Galette, 142
Raw Vegetable Salad with Açaí Vinaigrette, 52
Reese, Cheri, 80, 81
relish, sweet corn, 99

rhubarb
Beebopareebop Strawberry Rhubarb Cocktail, 78
Grilled Chicken with Rhubarb Barbecue Sauce, 98
Rosemary Rhubarb Jam, 143
rice
Gai Gai Thai Breakfast Bowl, 7–8
Sweet Corn Rice Pudding, 145
Wild Rice and Quinoa Porridge, 20
rice, wild
Squash and Wild Rice Chili, 73
Wild Rice and Quinoa Porridge, 20
Wild Rice Orzotto with Morels, Ramps, and Hazelnuts, 61
Wild Rice Salad with Maple-Toasted Almonds, 62
Roasted Beet Salad with Sherry Pepper Vinaigrette, 53
Roasted Cauliflower with Mint, Golden Raisins, Cornichons,
and Parmesan, 54–55
Roasted Chicken Thighs with Clams, Rapini, and Dill
Mayonnaise, 110–111
Roasted Garlic and Nettle Soup, 71
Roasted Ramps and Watercress with Pumpkin Seed Chèvre
Medallions, 56–57
Roasted Root Vegetables, 58
Roasted Squash and Sweet Potato Soup with Hazelnut Oil
and Saba, 72
Rosemary Rhubarb Jam, 143
rum
Får North Spirits Oak Island Rum Punch, 81
Russo, Lenny, 66–67, 99

S
salmon
Minnesota "Nice-oise" Salad with Salmon, 51
Salmon and Cheddar Quiche, 112–113
Salmon and Cheddar Quiche, 112–113
Salt Cellar, The 43, 94–95, 96–97, 149
Salty Tart, 144, 149
sandwiches
Pepito Ancho Butter and Pumpkin Jam Sandwiches, 106–107
sauces
bacon and arugula, 12–13
blueberry caramel, 134–136
coconut cream, 145
ginger-orange teriyaki, 120
Palisade Porter caramel, 123
Saunders, Don, 6, 129
sausage
Buttermilk Herb Biscuits and Chorizo-Poblano Gravy, 4–5
Savory Bread Pudding, 59
Savory Bread Pudding, 59
Scandinavian Inn, 3, 150
Schneider, Moni, 19, 76
Schoville, Justin, 54–55, 101–103
Seared Duck Breast and Amarena Cherries, 114–115
Sen Yai Sen Lek, 39, 118, 150
sesame
Pork Loin Katsu with Sesame Basil Pesto and Fingerling
Potato Confit, 108–109
Walleye with Sesame Crust and Ginger-Orange Teriyaki, 120
sherry
Roasted Beet Salad with Sherry Pepper Vinaigrette, 53

shortbread
Blueberry Bars with Lemon-Thyme Shortbread Crust, 124–125
slaw
Carrot-Family Slaw with Dill and Cilantro, 46
Grilled Bean Slaw, 48–49
Smoked Trout, Scrambled Eggs, Capers, and Trout Roe on Buttered
Toast, 36–37
Sofrito Potatoes, 60
Sommer Pasta, 116
sour cream
Green Gazpacho with Chive Sour Cream, 66–67
Honey-Vanilla Cheesecake with Blueberry Caramel Sauce,
134–136
Salmon and Cheddar Quiche, 112–113
Sofrito Potatoes, 60
Surly Furious Chocolate Bundt Cake, 144
Soused Herring, 38
spinach
Minnesota "Nice-oise" Salad with
Salmon, 51
Savory Bread Pudding, 59
Spoon and Stable Restaurant, 89–91, 150
Spoonriver, 120, 130–131, 150
squash, summer
Sommer Pasta, 116
squash, winter
Roasted Squash and Sweet Potato Soup
with Hazelnut Oil and Saba, 72
Squash and Wild Rice Chili, 73
Wild Hare Smoky Squash Chowder, 76
Squash and Wild Rice Chili, 73
Steady Eddie, 84
Stone, Sarah, 132
strawberries
Almond French Toast with Roasted Strawberry Jam
and Brown Sugar Cream, 2
Beebopareebop Strawberry Rhubarb Cocktail, 78
Surly Bender Braised Short Ribs, 117
Surly Furious Chocolate Bundt Cake, 144
Suss, Jason, 82
Swanson, Michael, 80, 81
Sweet Corn Rice Pudding, 145
Sweet Crispy Beef with Coriander Seed (Nuea Dat Deow), 118
sweet potatoes
Roasted Squash and Sweet Potato Soup with Hazelnut
Oil and Saba, 72
Seared Duck Breast and Amarena Cherries, 114–115
Swiss chard
Beef Wellington with Swiss Chard and Mushroom Duxelles, 86
Savory Bread Pudding, 59
syrup, rhubarb, 78

T
tacos
Tofu Veggie Breakfast Tacos, 18
tahini
Beet Hummus, 24
tarts
Plum Frangipane Tart, 140–141
Raspberry Galette, 142

teriyaki
    Walleye with Sesame Crust and Ginger-Orange Teriyaki, 120
Terzo, 64, 92–93, 150
That Food Girl, 23, 98
Thielen, Amy, 46, 122, 148
Third Bird, The, 2, 150
Three Crows, The, 150
Three Crows Minnesota Flappers, 17
Tod Mun Pla: Curried Fish Cakes with Cucumber Salad, 39
Tofu Veggie Breakfast Tacos, 18
tomatillos
    Green Gazpacho with Chive Sour Cream, 66–67
tomatoes
    Braised Beef Pot Roast, 88
    Braised Pork Shank Ossobuco with Herb Gremolata
        (Ossobuco di Maiale), 92–93
    Broccoli and Sun-dried Tomato Quiche, 3
    Fried Green Tomatoes with Skillet Sweet Corn Vinaigrette, 29–31
    Lemongrass Pork Tenderloin over Mixed Greens, 50
    Prairie Bay's BYOB (Build Your Own Bruschetta), 34–35
    Squash and Wild Rice Chili, 73
    Tomato-Fennel Soup with "Inside Out" Grilled Cheese
        Sandwiches, 74–75
    Wild Hare Cuban Breakfast Burritos, 19
Tomato-Fennel Soup with "Inside Out" Grilled Cheese Sandwiches,
    74–75
tomato sauce
    Maple Stout Sloppy Joes, 105
Tongue in Cheek, 25, 137–138, 150
Torkelson, Peter, 3
Torkelson, Vicki Chambard, 3
tortillas
    Tofu Veggie Breakfast Tacos, 18
    Wild Hare Cuban Breakfast Burritos, 19
trout
    Lake Superior Trout and Pumpkin Chowder, 63, 70
    Smoked Trout, Scrambled Eggs, Capers, and Trout Roe
        on Buttered Toast, 36–37
True Cost Farm, 32, 150
truffles
    Goat Cheese, Honey, Date, and Pistachio Truffles, 133
turkey
    Brined Turkey with Pan Jus and Caramelized Salsify, 94–95
turnips
    Roasted Root Vegetables, 58
turnovers
    Apple and Smoked Gouda Turnovers, 22

V
vegetable broth
    Wild Hare Smoky Squash Chowder, 76
vegetables, mixed
    Wild Hare Cuban Breakfast Burritos, 19
vegetable stock
    Charred Bell Pepper Soup with Chèvre and Balsamic Vinegar, 64
    Lake Superior Trout and Pumpkin Chowder, 63, 70
    Roasted Squash and Sweet Potato Soup with Hazelnut Oil
        and Saba, 72
    Tomato-Fennel Soup with "Inside Out" Grilled Cheese
        Sandwiches, 74–75
    Wild Rice Orzotto with Morels, Ramps, and Hazelnuts, 61

Venison Tenderloin with Miso Sauce, 119
Vickerman, Adam, 58, 88
Victory 44, 74–75, 126–127, 150
Vikre, Emily, 78, 83
Vikre Distillery, 78, 83, 150
vinaigrettes, 29–31, 52, 53
Vollom, Daniel, 117, 134–136
Voyageur Brewing Beer Cheese Fondue, 40
Voyageur Brewing Company, 40, 123, 150

W
walleye
    Tod Mun Pla: Curried Fish Cakes with Cucumber Salad, 39
    Walleye with Sesame Crust and Ginger-Orange Teriyaki, 120
Walleye with Sesame Crust and Ginger-Orange Teriyaki, 120
Waves of Superior Cafe, 61, 150
Wedge & Wheel, The, 133, 150
whipping cream
    Whiskey Honey Cake with Whiskey Whipped Cream
        Filling, 121, 146
whiskey
    Sweet Crispy Beef with Coriander Seed (Nuea Dat Deow), 118
    Whiskey Honey Cake with Whiskey Whipped Cream
        Filling, 121, 146
Whiskey Honey Cake with Whiskey Whipped Cream
    Filling, 121, 146
Wild Hare Bistro, 19, 76, 150
Wild Hare Cuban Breakfast Burritos, 19
Wild Hare Smoky Squash Chowder, 76
Wild Rice and Quinoa Porridge, 20
Wild Rice Orzotto with Morels, Ramps, and Hazelnuts, 61
Wild Rice Salad with Maple-Toasted Almonds, 62
wine
    Braised Beef Pot Roast, 88
    Braised Pork Shank Ossobuco with Herb Gremolata
        (Ossobuco di Maiale), 92–93
    Brined Turkey with Pan Jus and Caramelized Salsify, 94–95
    Buttered Popcorn Gnocchi with Port Wine Reduction, 41, 44–45
    Charred Bell Pepper Soup with Chèvre and Balsamic Vinegar, 64
    Grilled Corn and Potato Chowder, 68–69
    Lamb Chops with Spring Vegetables, 100
    Norseman Strawberry Rhubarb Fizz, 82
    Prairie Bay's BYOB (Build Your Own Bruschetta), 34–35
    Roasted Chicken Thighs with Clams, Rapini, and Dill
        Mayonnaise, 110–111
    Roasted Garlic and Nettle Soup, 71
    Squash and Wild Rice Chili, 73
Wise Acre Eatery, 24, 29–31, 150
Wong, Tammy, 50, 145

Y
yogurt
    Fermented Herb Yogurt Dip, 28
    Green Goddess Dressing, 47

Z
Zimmern, Andrew, 119
Zoë Bakes, 124–125, 150
Zzest Café, 54–55, 101–103, 105